ROMAN GODS & GODDESSES

GODS AND GODDESSES OF MYTHOLOGY

ROMAN GODS & GODDESSES

EDITED BY WILLIAM WHITE

Britannica®
Educational Publishing

IN ASSOCIATION WITH

ROSEN
EDUCATIONAL SERVICES

Published in 2014 by Britannica Educational Publishing (a trademark of Encyclopædia Britannica, Inc.) in association with The Rosen Publishing Group, Inc.
29 East 21st Street, New York, NY 10010

Distributed exclusively by Rosen Publishing.
To see additional Britannica Educational Publishing titles, go to
http://www.rosenpublishing.com

First Edition

Britannica Educational Publishing
J. E. Luebering: Director, Core Reference Group
Anthony L. Green: Editor, Compton's by Britannica

Rosen Publishing
Hope Lourie Killcoyne: Executive Editor
Nicholas Croce: Editor
William White: Editor
Nelson Sá: Art Director
Cindy Reiman: Photography Manager
Nicole Baker: Photo Researcher

Cataloging-in-Publication Data

White, William.
Roman gods & goddesses/edited by William White—1st ed.
        p. cm.—(Gods & goddesses of mythology)
"In association with Britannica Educational Publishing, Rosen Educational Services."
Includes index and bibliography.
ISBN 978-1-62275-158-7 (library binding)
1. Gods, Roman—Juvenile literature. 2. Mythology, Roman—Juvenile literature.
3. Rome—Religious life and customs—Juvenile literature. I. Title.
BL803.W55 2014
292.2—d23

Manufactured in the United States of America

On the cover: Statue of Neptune in the Fontana del Nettuno (Fountain of Neptune) in Rome, Italy. © iStockphoto.com/wjarek

Interior pages (mosaic) © iStockphoto.com/Fyletto; back cover © iStockphoto.com/ DavidMSchrader

CONTENTS

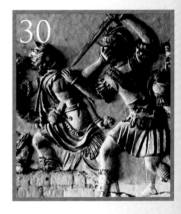

The Pantheon in Rome, Italy, was built during the reign of Augustus as the temple to all the gods of ancient Rome. Sergey Kelin/Shutterstock.com

INTRODUCTION

The Romans, according to the orator and politician Cicero, excelled all other peoples in the unique wisdom that made them realize that everything is subordinate to the rule and direction of the gods. Yet Roman religion was based not on divine grace but on mutual trust (fides) between god and man. The object of Roman religion was to secure the cooperation, benevolence, and peace of the gods (pax deorum). The Romans believed that this divine help would make it possible for them to master the unknown forces around them that inspired awe and anxiety (religio), and thus they would be able to live successfully. Consequently, there arose a body of rules, the *jus divinum* ("divine law"), ordaining what had to be done or avoided.

These precepts for many centuries contained scarcely any moral element; they consisted of directions for the correct performance of ritual. Roman religion laid almost exclusive emphasis on cult acts, endowing them with all the sanctity of patriotic tradition. Roman ceremonial was so obsessively meticulous and conservative that, if the various partisan accretions that grew upon it throughout the years can be eliminated, remnants of very early thought can be detected near the surface.

This demonstrates one of the many differences between Roman religion and Greek religion, in which such remnants tend to be deeply concealed. The Greeks, when they first began to document themselves, had already gone quite a long way toward sophisticated, abstract, and sometimes daring conceptions of divinity and its relation to man. But the orderly, legalistic, and relatively inarticulate Romans never quite gave up their old practices. Moreover, until the vivid pictorial imagination of the Greeks began to influence them, they lacked the Greek taste for seeing their deities in personalized human form and endowing them with mythology. In a

Statue of Cicero at the Palazzo di Giustizia (Palace of Justice) in Rome, Italy. Hemera/Thinkstock

sense, there is no Roman mythology, or scarcely any. Although discoveries in the 20th century, notably in the ancient region of Etruria (between the Tiber and Arno rivers, west and south of the Apennines), confirm that Italians were not entirely unmythological, their mythology is sparse. What is found in Rome is chiefly a pseudomythology (which, in due course, clothed their own nationalistic or family legends in mythical dress borrowed from the Greeks). Nor did Roman religion have a creed; provided that a Roman performed the right religious actions, he was free to think what he liked about the gods. And, having no creed, he usually deprecated emotion as out of place in acts of worship.

However, in spite of the antique features not far from the surface, it is difficult to reconstruct the history and evolution of Roman religion. The principal literary sources, antiquarians such as the 1st-century BCE Roman scholars Varro and Verrius Flaccus, and the poets who were their contemporaries (under the late Republic and Augustus), wrote 700 and 800 years after the beginnings of Rome. They wrote at a time when the introduction of Greek methods and myths had made erroneous (and flattering) interpretations of the distant Roman past unavoidable. In order to supplement such conjectures or facts as they may provide, scholars rely on surviving copies of the religious calendar and on other inscriptions. There is also a rich, though frequently cryptic, treasure-house of material in coins and medallions and in works of art.

CHAPTER 1

ROMAN HISTORY

For the earliest times, there are the various finds and findings of archaeology. But they are not sufficient to enable scholars to reconstruct archaic Roman religion. They do, however, suggest that early in the 1st millennium BCE, though not necessarily at the time of the traditional date for the founding of Rome (753 BCE), Latin and Sabine shepherds and farmers with light plows came from the Alban Hills and the Sabine Hills, and that they proceeded to establish villages in Rome, the Latins on the Palatine Hill and the Sabines (though this is uncertain) on the Quirinal and Esquiline hills. About 620, the communities merged, and *c.* 575 the Forum Romanum between them became the town's meeting place and market.

DEIFICATION OF FUNCTIONS

From such evidence it appears that the early Romans, like many other Italians, sometimes saw divine force, or divinity, operating in pure function and act, such as in human activities like opening doors or giving birth to children, and in nonhuman phenomena such as the movements of the sun and seasons of the soil. They directed this feeling of veneration both toward happenings that affected human beings regularly and, sometimes, toward single, unique manifestations, such as a mysterious voice that once spoke and saved them in a crisis (Aius Locutius). They multiplied functional deities of this kind to an extraordinary degree of "religious

Ancient Roman boundary stone. DEA/A. Dagli Orti/De Agostini/ Getty Images

atomism," in which countless powers or forces were identified with one phase of life or another. Their functions were sharply defined, and in approaching them it was important to use their right names and titles. If one knew the name, one could secure a hearing. Failing that, it was often best to cover every contingency by

13

admitting that the divinity was "unknown" or adding the precautionary phrase "or whatever name you want to be called" or "if it be a god or goddess."

To describe the powers in these objects and functions that inspired the horror, or sacred thrill, the Romans eventually employed the word *numen*, suggestive of a god's nod, nutus; though so far there is no evidence that this usage was earlier than the 2nd century BCE. The application of the word *spirit* to numen is anachronistic in regard to early epochs because it presupposes a society capable of greater abstraction. Nor must the term *mana*, used by Melanesians to describe their own concept of superhuman forces, be introduced too readily. The two societies are not necessarily analogous and, besides, the deduction from such comparisons that the Romans experienced an impersonal, pre-deistic, primordial stage of religion that neatly preceded the personal stage cannot be regarded as correct. On the contrary, from the very earliest times, the supernatural forces that they envisaged included a number of deities in analogous human forms; among them were certain "high gods." Foremost among these was a divinity of the sky, Jupiter, akin

Illustration of Julius Caesar refusing the crown from Mark Antony during the Lupercalia festival. Archive Photos/ Hulton Royals Collection/Getty Images

to the sky gods of other early Indo-European-speaking peoples, the Sanskrit Dyaus and Greek Zeus. Not yet, probably, a Supreme Being, though superior in some sense to other divine powers, this god of the heavens was easily linked with the forces of function and object, with lightning and weather, or with the uncanny stone that came from on high and was called Jupiter Lapis.

RELIGION IN THE ETRUSCAN PERIOD

The apparent amalgamation of the Latin and Sabine villages of Rome coincided with, or more probably was soon followed by, a period in which Rome was under the control of at least one dynasty (the Tarquins) from Etruria, north of the Tiber (c. 575–510 BCE, though some scholars would extend this domination to c. 450).

IMPORTANCE OF RITUAL

The Etruscans felt profound religious anxieties and were more devoted to ritual than any other people of the ancient Western world. Though sources are, again, late and unsatisfactory, it appears that they possessed a comprehensive collection of rules regulating these rites. Etruscan culture was heavily based on influences from Greece in its orientalizing period, conveyed mainly through Greek centres (such as Cumae) in Campania, colonized by Euboeans, who were also prominent in Syrian markets. But the religion of Etruria proclaims a very un-Greek view of the abasement and nonentity of man before the gods and their will.

To the Etruscans the whole fanatical effort of life was directed toward forcing their deities, led by Tinia or Tin (Jupiter), to yield up their secrets by divination. They saw an intimate link existing between heaven and Earth, which seemed to echo one another within a unitary system, and they were more ambitious than either Greeks or Romans in their claims to foretell the future. They also formed an exceptionally complex, rich, and imaginative picture of the afterlife. The living were perpetually obsessed by their care for the dead, expressed in elaborate, magnificently equipped and decorated tombs and lavish sacrifices. For, in spite of beliefs in an underworld, or Hades, there was also a conviction that the individuality of the dead somehow continued in their mortal remains; and it was therefore imperative that they take pleasure in their graves or tombs and not return to haunt the living. From the 4th century BCE onward, after the Etruscans had lost their political power to Rome, their art depicts horrors indicating an increasing fear of what death might bring.

INFLUENCE ON ROMAN RELIGION

The Roman religion continued to display certain obvious debts to the period when the city had been under Etruscan control. It is true that the Roman shades (Di Manes) were much less substantial than the fantastic Etruscan conceptions and, although Etruscan divination by the liver and entrails survived and later became increasingly fashionable in Rome, Roman diviners in general, products of a more realistic and prosaic society, never aspired to such precise information about the future as the Etruscans had hoped to gain. Yet, it was the Etruscans who first gave a vigorous definition to Italian religious forms. Indeed, many of the religious features that patriotic historians preferred to ascribe to the mythical King Numa Pompilius (who was supposed to have been Romulus's Sabine successor in the 8th century BCE—the man of peace following the man of war) date, in fact, from the period of Etruscan

16

domination two centuries later. Nevertheless, Romans acknowledged a debt to Etruria that included much ceremony and ritual and the plan, appearance, and decoration of a number of temples, notably the great shrine of the Capitoline Triad, Jupiter, Juno, and Minerva. The Romans also were indebted to the Etruscans for their first statues of gods, including the cult image of Jupiter commissioned from an Etruscan for the Capitoline temple. Such statuary, showing the gods in human shape, encouraged the Romans to think of their gods in this way, with the consequent possibility of investing them with myths, which thereafter gradually accumulated around them in the form of Hellenic stories often infused with a native patriotic element.

Denarii with portraits of Titus Tatius and Numa Pompilius. Iberfoto/SuperStock

Above all, Rome owed to its Etruscan kings its religious calendar. In addition to poetical works discussing the calendar in antiquarian fashion, such as the *Fasti* of Ovid, there are extant fragments of about 40 copies of the calendar itself, in a revised shape established by Julius Caesar. Besides the Julian revision, there is an incomplete pre-Caesarian, Republican calendar, the Fasti Antiates, discovered at Antium (Anzio); it dates from after 100 BCE. It is possible to detect in

17

these calendars much that is very ancient, including a pre-Etruscan 10-month solar year. However, the basis of the calendars, in their surviving form, is later, since it consists of an attempt to reconcile the solar and lunar year, in accordance with Babylonian calculations. This endeavour belongs to the period of Etruscan domination of Rome—for example, the names of the months April and June (in their Roman form) come from Etruria. Moreover, the presence or absence of certain festivals permits a dating approximating to the time of Etruscan domination in the later 6th century BCE. Additional modifications were introduced in the following century and again when the calendar was subsequently published (30 BCE).

The festivals it records, of which the earliest are indicated in large letters, reflect a period of transition between country and town life. Though local cult continued to remain active, many forms of worship hitherto maintained by families and farms had now been taken over by the comparatively mature Roman state. The state management blocked any tendency toward spiritualization and removed the need for any vigorous individual participation; however, by ensuring that the gods were conciliated by a schedule corresponding to the regular process of nature, it made the individual citizens feel for centuries that relations with the supernatural were being maintained safely.

RELIGION IN THE EARLY REPUBLIC

Even if, as tradition records, a coup d'état dislodged the Etruscan kings before 500 BCE, in the first half of the 5th century there was no weakening of trade relations with Etruria. Its southern cities, such as Caere (Cerveteri) and Veii close to Rome, had long used the Greek city of Cumae

Greek city of Cumae. Marka/SuperStock

as a commercial outlet, converting it into an important grain supplier. And now Rome, faced with a shortage of grain, arranged for it to be imported from Cumae. The same city also influenced the foundation of Roman temples in the Greek style. Rome, which had already become accustomed to Greek religious customs in the Etruscan epoch, now showed a willingness to absorb them. This forms a strange contrast to its deeply ingrained religious conservatism. Moreover, at some quite early stage (though there is no positive evidence of the practice until the 3rd century), Romans borrowed from elsewhere in Italy a special ritual (evocatio) for inviting the patron deities of captured towns to abandon their homes and migrate to Rome.

In an emergency in 399 BCE, during a difficult siege of Veii, Rome carried Hellenization further by importing a Greek rite in which, as an appeal to emotional feeling, images of pairs of gods were exhibited on couches before tables spread with food and drink; this rite (lectisternium) was designed to make them Rome's welcome guests. From the same century onward, if not earlier, pestilences were averted by another ritual (supplicatio), in which the whole populace went around the temples and prostrated themselves in Greek fashion. Later the custom was extended to the celebration of victories.

RELIGION IN THE LATER REPUBLIC: CRISES AND NEW TRENDS

The lectisternium was repeated, with increased elaboration and pomp, in 217 BCE during a period in which emotional religion was running rampant because of Hannibal's invasion of Italy in the Second Punic War. Faced with a flood of fears and anxieties and reports of many alarming and extraordinary events, Rome took precautions to secure the favour of all manner of gods. Among them, as a desperate attempt at novelty when appeals to the usual deities seemed stale, was the introduction of the Great Mother of Asia Minor, Cybele (204 BCE). Eighteen years later, the equally orgiastic worship of Dionysus (Bacchus) was coming in so rapidly and violently, by way of southern Italy, that the Senate, scenting subversion, repressed its practitioners. But these and other mystery religions, promising initiation, afterlife, and an excitement that Roman national cults could not provide, had come to stay and, although there were long periods of official disapproval before acclimatization was completed, they gradually played an immense part upon the religious scene. Eastern astrology, too, became extremely popular. It was based on the conviction that, since there is cosmic sympathy between Earth and other heavenly bodies, and since, therefore, the emanations of these bodies influence Earth, men must learn how to foresee their dictates—and outwit them.

Astrological practices received encouragement from Stoic philosophy, which was introduced to Rome in the 2nd and early 1st centuries BCE, notably by Panaetius and Poseidonius. The Stoics saw this pseudoscience as proof of the Platonic unity of the universe. Stoicism affected Roman religious thinking in at least three other ways. First, it had a deterministic effect, encouraging a widespread belief in Fate and also, somewhat illogically, in

Third-century CE *mosaic depicting a scene by comic dramatist Plautus.* DEA Picture Library/De Agostini/Getty Images

21

Fortune, both of which were revered in other parts of the Mediterranean and Middle Eastern world. Second, Stoicism infused a new spirituality into religious thinking by its insistence that the human soul is part of the universal spirit and shares its divinity. Third, the moral implication of this, as the Stoics pointed out, was that all men are brothers and must treat each other accordingly. This demonstration struck a chord in the psychology of the Romans, who possessed strongly ethical inclinations and now, at last, saw this trend supported and justified by a philosophical sanction that their formalistic religion had not provided. In changing times of imperialism, materialism, and widespread heart-searching, the state religion had failed to fill the vacuum, and philosophy stepped in instead. At the same time the negative approach of Roman religion to the afterlife was counteracted by an influx of speculations that blended theology, mysticism, and magic and claimed the mythical Orpheus and the part historical, part legendary Pythagoras as prophets.

While their national poet Ennius helped to diffuse such beliefs, he and the comic dramatist Plautus ridiculed the traditional Roman gods on the stage. The upper-class attitude of the times was expressed by the historian Polybius, the priestly lawyer Scaevola, the scholarly Varro, and the orator and philosopher Cicero, who maintained that the importance of religion was political, residing in its power to keep the multitude under control, to prevent social chaos, and to promote patriotic feeling.

THE IMPERIAL EPOCH: THE FINAL FORMS OF ROMAN PAGANISM

After the prolonged horrors of civil war had ended (30 BCE), the victorious Octavian, the adoptive son of the dictator Caesar and founder of the imperial regime or principate, decided, correctly, that the ancient religion was far from dead and that the restoration of all its forms would respond to a strong popular, instinctive belief that the disasters of the past generations had been due to the neglect of religious duties.

THE IMPERIAL CULT

Octavian himself took the name *Augustus*, a term indicating a claim to reverence. This did not make him a god in his lifetime, but, combined with the insertion of his numen and his genius (originally the procreative power that enables a family to be carried on) into certain cults, it prepared the way for his posthumous deification, just as Caesar had been deified before him. Both were deified by the state because they seemed to have given Rome gifts worthy of a god. From earliest times in Greece there had been an idea that, if someone saved you, you should pay him the honours you would offer to a god. Alexander the Great and his successors had demanded reverence as divine saviours, and Ptolemy II Philadelphus of Egypt introduced a cult of his own living person. The Stoic belief that the human soul was part of the world soul was a corollary of the view that great men possessed a larger share of this divine element. Moreover, the 3rd-century BCE mythographer Euhemerus had elaborated a theory that the gods themselves had once been human; this idea was readily adapted to the supposed careers of Heracles (Hercules) and the Dioscuri (Castor and Polydeuces [Pollux]); and the Romans applied it to their own gods Saturn and Quirinus, the latter identified with the national founder, Romulus, risen to heaven. And so it became customary—if emperors (and empresses) were approved of in their lives—to raise them to divinity after their deaths. They were called divi, not dei like the Olympian gods; the latter were prayed to, but the former were regarded with veneration and gratitude.

As the empire proceeded and the old religion seemed more and more irrelevant to people's personal preoccupations and successive national emergencies, the cult of the divi, subsequently grouped together in a single Hall of Fame, remained foremost among the patriotic cults that were increasingly encouraged as unifying forces. Concentrating on the protectors of the emperor and the nation, they included the worship of Rome herself, and of the genius of the Roman people; for the army a number of special military celebrations are recorded on the Calendar of Doura-Europos in Mesopotamia (Feriale Duranum, *c.* 225–27 CE). As for the ruling emperors, they were more and more frequently treated as divine, with varying degrees of formality, and

Cliffs of Doura-Europos on the banks of the Euphrates. Yves Gellie/Gamma-Rapho/Getty Images

officially they often were compared with gods. As monotheistic tendencies grew, however, this custom led not so much to their identification with the gods as to the doctrine that they were the elect of the divine powers, who were defined as their companions (comites). In pursuance of this way of thinking, as official paganism approached its last days, the emperors Diocletian and Maximian took the names Jovius and Herculius, respectively, after their Companions and Patrons Jupiter and Hercules.

Introduction of Christianity and Mithraism

By now, however, the humanistic idea that men could become gods had ceased to have any plausibility. Plotinus and his Neoplatonism, the dominant philosophy of the pagan world from the mid-3rd century CE, had given powerful, mystical shape to the Platonic and Stoic conception that the universe is governed by a single force. On the other hand, the greatest religious figure of the century, the Iranian Mani, who had started to preach in Mesopotamia c. 240, dramatically preached the opposing dualistic idea that the world is the creation not only of a good power but of an evil one as well. Mani's church, which alarmed Diocletian and for a time attracted the great Christian theologian St. Augustine, absorbed many of the innumerable cults of Gnostics who claimed special knowledge (gnosis) by illumination and revelation and taught how people can purge the nonspiritual from within themselves and escape their earthly prison. More impressively, the cult of the Persian Mithra blended the dualism of Mani with the emotional initiations of the mystery religions (corrected by a much sterner tone of moral endeavour) and became a strong link between the cult of the Sun (which appealed to contemporary monotheists) and the fashionable revulsion from the senses that was shortly to lead to Christian monasticism. Like Christianity, Mithraism had its sacraments; but the life of Mithra exercised a less far-reaching appeal than the life of Christ, and Mithra's cult excluded women.

Christianity, unique in its universal charity and unique also in its demand for a noble effort of faith in Jesus's blend of divinity and humanity, was the religion that prevailed in the Roman world. It satisfied the emperor Constantine's impulsive need for divine support, and from 312 CE onward, by a complex and gradual process, it became the official religion of the empire.

THE SURVIVAL OF ROMAN RELIGION

For a time, coins and other monuments continued to link Christian doctrines with the worship of the Sun, to which Constantine had been addicted previously. But even when this phase came to an end, Roman paganism continued to exert other, permanent influences, great and small. The emperors passed on to the popes the title of chief priest, pontifex maximus. The saints, with their distribution of functions, often seemed to perpetuate the many numina of ancient tradition. The ecclesiastical calendar retains numerous remnants of pre-Christian festivals—notably Christmas, which blends elements including both the feast of the Saturnalia and the birthday of Mithra. But, most of all, the mainstream of Western Christianity owed ancient Rome the firm discipline that gave it stability and shape, combining insistence on established forms with the possibility of recognizing that novelties need not be excluded, since they were implicit from the start.

BELIEFS, PRACTICES, AND INSTITUTIONS

CHAPTER 2

The early Romans, like other Italians, worshiped not only purely functional and local forces but also certain high gods. Chief among them was the sky god Jupiter, whose cult, at first limited to the communities around the Alban Hills, later gained Rome as an adherent. The Romans gave Jupiter his own priest (flamen), and the fact that there were two other senior flamines, devoted to Mars and Quirinus, confirms other indications that the cults of these three deities, envisaged perhaps in some sort of association, belonged to a very early stratum (though the theory of their correspondence to the three-class social division of the early Indo-European-speaking peoples is generally unacceptable). Mars, whose name may or may not be Indo-European, was a high god of many Italian peoples, as liturgical bronze tablets found at Iguvium (Gubbio), the Tabulae Iguvinae (c. 200–c. 80 BCE), confirm, protecting them in war and defending their agriculture and animals against disease. Later, he was identified with the Greek god of war, Ares, and was regarded as the father of Romulus. Mars Gradivus presided over the beginning of a war and Mars Quirinus over its end, but earlier Quirinus had apparently, as a separate deity, been the patron of the Quirinal village before its amalgamation with the Palatine; subsequently he was believed to have been the god that Romulus became when he ascended into heaven.

Two other forces that belong to an early phase were Janus and Vesta, the powers of the door and hearth, respectively. Janus, who had no Greek equivalent, was worshiped beside the Forum in a small shrine with double doors at either end and originated either from a divine power that regulated the passage over running water or rather, perhaps, from sacred doorways like those found on the art of Bronze Age Mycenae. Janus originally stood for the magic of the door of a private house or hut and later became a part of the state religion. The gates of his temple were formally closed when the state was at peace, a custom going back to the primitive war magic that required armies to march out to battle by this properly sanctified route. Vesta, too, passed from the home to the state, always retaining a circular temple reminiscent of the primitive huts whose form can be reconstructed from traces left in the earth and from surviving funerary urns. Vesta's shrine contained the eternal fire, but the absence of a statue indicates that it preceded the anthropomorphic period; its correspondence with the Indian garhapatya, "house-father's fire," suggest an origin prior to the time of the differentiation of the Indo-European-speaking peoples. The cultic site just outside the area of the primitive Palatine settlement indicates that there had been a form of fire worship even earlier than Vesta's (dedicated to the deity Caca) on the Palatine itself. The cult of Vesta, tended by her Virgins, continued to flourish until the end of antiquity, endowed with an important role in the sacred protectorship of Rome.

The *Di Manes*, collective powers (later "spirits") of the dead, may mean "the good people," an anxious euphemism like the Greek name of "the kindly ones" for the Furies. As a member of the family or clan, however, the dead man or woman would, more specifically, be one of the *Di Parentes*; reverence for ancestors was the core of Roman religious and social life. *Di Indigetes* was a name given collectively to these forebears, as well as to other deified powers or spirits who likewise controlled the destiny of Rome. For example, the name *Indiges* is applied to Aeneas, whose mythical immigration from Troy led to the eventual foundation of the city. According to an inscription of the 4th century BCE (found at Tor Tignosa, 15 miles south of Rome), Aeneas is also called Lar, which indicates that the Lares, too, were originally regarded as divine ancestors and not as deities who presided over the farmland. The Lares were worshiped wherever properties adjoined, and inside every home their statuettes were placed in the domestic shrine (lararium). Under state control they moved from boundaries of properties to crossroads (where Augustus eventually associated his own genius with the cult) and were worshiped as the guardian spirits of the whole community (Lares Praestites). The cult of the Di Penates likewise moved from house to state. From very early times the Penates, the powers that ensured that there was enough to eat, were worshiped in every home. They also came to be regarded as national protectors, the Penates Publici. Originally they were synonymous with the Dioscuri. The legend that they had been brought to Italy by Aeneas with his followers from Troy was imported from Lavinium (Pratica di Mare) when the early Romans incorporated that town into their own state.

THE DIVINITIES OF THE LATER REGAL PERIOD

Two other deities whose Roman cults tradition attributed to the period of the kings were Diana and Fors Fortuna. Diana, an Italian wood goddess worshiped at Aricia (Ariccia) in Latium and prayed to by women who wanted children, was in due course identified with the Greek Artemis. Her temple on the Aventine Hill (c. 540 BCE) with its statue, an imitation of a Greek model from Massilia (Marseille), was based on the Temple of Artemis

Stucco relief by Antonio Melana of the assasination of Servius Tullius, located in the Castle of Kratochvile, Czech Republic. Alinari Archives/ Getty Images

of Ephesus. By establishing such a sanctuary, the Roman monarch Servius Tullius hoped to emulate the Pan-Ionian League among the Latin peoples. Fors Fortuna, whose temple across the Tiber from the city was one of the few that slaves could attend, was similar to the oracular shrines of Fortuna at Antium (Anzio) and Praeneste (Palestrina). Originally a farming deity, she eventually represented luck. She came to be identified with Tyche, the patroness of cities and goddess of Fortune among the Hellenistic Greeks.

In Roman tradition, Servius Tullius reigned between two Etruscan kings, Tarquinius Priscus and Tarquinius Superbus. The Etruscan kings began and perhaps finished the most important Roman temple, devoted to the cult of the Capitoline Triad, Jupiter, Juno, and Minerva (the dedication was believed to have taken place in 509 or 507 BCE after the expulsion of the Etruscans). Such triads, housed in temples with three chambers (cellae), were an Etruscan institution. But the grouping of these three Roman deities seems to be owed to Greek anthropomorphic ideas, since Hera and Athena, with whom Juno and Minerva were identified, were respectively the wife and daughter of Zeus (Jupiter). In Italy, Juno (Uni in Etruscan) was sometimes the war-like high goddess of a town (e.g., Lanuvium [Lanuvio] in Latium), but her chief function was to supervise the life of women, and particularly their sexual life. The functions of Minerva concerned craftsmen and reflected the growing industrial life of Rome. Two gods with Etruscan names, both worshiped at open altars before they had temples in Rome, were Vulcan and Saturn, the former a fire god identified with the Greek blacksmiths' deity Hephaestus, and the latter an agricultural god identified with Cronus, the father of Zeus. Saturn was worshiped in Greek fashion, with head uncovered.

The focal point of the cult of Hercules was the Great Altar (Ara Maxima) in the cattle market, just inside the boundaries of the primitive Palatine settlement. The altar may be traced to a shrine of Melkart established by traders from Phoenicia in the 7th century BCE. The name of the god, however, was derived from the Greek Heracles, whose worship spread northward from southern Italy, brought by traders who venerated his journeys, his labours, and his power to avert evil. In a market frequented by strangers, a widely recognized divinity of this type was needed to keep the peace. The Greek cult, at first private, perhaps dates from the 5th century BCE.

The Divinities of the Republic

An important series of temples was founded early in the 5th century BCE. The completion of the temple of the Etruscan Saturn was attributed to this time (497). A shrine honouring the twin horsemen, the Dioscuri (Castor and Pollux), was also built in this period. An inscription from Lavinium describing them by the Greek term *kouroi* indicates a Greek origin (from southern Italy) without Etruscan mediation. In legend, the Dioscuri had helped Rome to victory in a battle against the Latins at Lake Regillus, and in historic times, on anniversaries of that engagement, they continued to preside over the annual parade of knights (equites). From southern Italy, too, came the cult of Ceres, whose temple traditionally was vowed in 496 and dedicated in 493. Ceres was an old Italian deity who presided over the generative powers of nature and came to be identified with Demeter, the Greek goddess of grain. She owed her installation in Rome to the influence of the Greek colony of Cumae, from which the Romans imported grain during a threatened famine. The association of Ceres at this temple with two other deities, Liber (a fertility god identified with Dionysus) and Libera (his female counterpart), was based on the triad at Eleusis in Greece. The Roman temple, built in the Etruscan style but with Greek ornamentation, stood beside a Greek trading centre on the Aventine Hill and became a rallying ground for the plebeians, the humbler section of the community who were hard hit by the grain shortage at this time and who were pressing for their rights against the patricians.

Cumae also played a part in the introduction of Apollo. The Sibylline oracles housed in Apollo's shrine at Cumae allegedly were brought to Rome by the last Etruscan kings. The importation of the cult (431 BCE) was prescribed by the Sibylline Books at a time when Rome, as on earlier occasions, had requested Cumae for help with grain. The Cumaean Apollo, however, was primarily prophetic, whereas the Roman cult, introduced at a time of epidemic, was concerned principally with his gifts as a healer. This role may possibly have been derived from the Etruscans, whose Apollo is known from a superb statue of c. 500 BCE from Veii, Etruria's nearest city to Rome. In 82 BCE the Sibylline Books were destroyed and replaced by a collection assembled from various sources. Later, Augustus elevated Apollo as the patron of himself and his regime, intending thereby to convert the brilliant Hellenic god of peace and civilization to the glory of Rome.

Unlike Apollo, Aphrodite did not keep her name when she became identified with an Italian deity. Instead, she took on the name Venus, derived, without complete certainty, from the idea of venus, "blooming nature" (the derivation from venia, "grace," seems less likely). She gained greatly in significance because of the legend that she was the mother of Aeneas, the ancestor of Rome, whom statuettes of the 5th century BCE from Veii show escaping from Troy with his father and son. From the time of the Punic Wars 200 years later the Trojan legend grew, for long before the 1st-century BCE dictators Sulla and Caesar claimed Venus as their ancestor, the story was interpreted as the preface to the Carthaginian struggle.

A number of gods were spoken of as possessing accompaniments, often in the feminine gender; e.g., Lua Saturni and Moles Martis. These attachments, sometimes spoken of as cult partners, were not the wives of the male divinities but rather expressed a special aspect of their power or will. A similar origin could be ascribed to the worship of divine powers representing "qualities." Fides ("Faith" or "Loyalty"), for example, may at first have been an attribute or aspect of a Latin-Sabine god of oaths, Semo Sanctus Dius Fidius; and in the same way Victoria may come from Jupiter Victor. Some of these concepts were worshiped very early, such as Ops ("Plenty," later associated with Saturn and equated with Hebe), and Juventas (who watched over the men of military age). The first of these qualities to receive a temple, as far as is known, is Concordia (367), in celebration of the end of civil strife. Salus (health or well-being) followed in c. 302, Victoria in c. 300, Pietas (dutifulness to family and gods, later exalted by Virgil as the whole basis of Roman religion) in 191. The Greeks, too, from the earliest days, had clothed such qualities in words; e.g., Shame, Peace, Justice, and Fortune. In the Hellenic world they had a wide variety of signification, ranging from full-fledged divinity to nothing more than abstractions. But in early Rome and Italy they were in no sense abstractions or allegories and were likewise not thought of as possessing the anthropomorphic shape that the term *personification* might imply. They were things, objects of worship, like many other functions that were venerated. They were external divine forces working upon humans and affecting them with the qualities that their names described. Later on, under philosophical (particularly Stoic) influences that flooded into ethically minded Rome, they duly took their place as moral concepts, the Virtues and Blessings that abounded for centuries and were depicted in human form on Roman coinage as part of the imperial propaganda.

THE SUN AND STARS

Little or no contribution to cosmology was made in the Roman world, and the demonstration of Aristarchus of Samos (c. 270 BCE) that Earth revolves around the Sun received virtually no support. The complicated geocentric interpretation that held sway in Rome was summed up in Cicero's *Dream of Scipio*. It formed the basis for the concept of the solar system on which the popular pseudoscience of astrology was founded, the Sun being regarded as the centre of the concentric planetary spheres encircling Earth—not the centre of the cosmos in the sense of Aristarchus but its heart. From the 5th century BCE onward this solar god was identified with Apollo in his role as the supreme dispenser of agricultural wealth. Possessor of a sacred grove at Lavinium, Sol Indiges was regarded as one of the divine ancestors of Rome. During the last centuries before the Christian era, worship of the Sun spread throughout the Mediterranean world and formed the principal rallying point of paganism's last years. Closely associated with the sun cult was that of Mithra, the Sun's ally and agent who was elevated to partake of communion and the love feast as the god's companion. Sun worship was popular in the army, and particularly on the Danube. Aurelian, one of the great military emperors produced by that area in the 3rd century, built a magnificent temple of Sol Invictus (the

"Unconquered Sun") at Rome (274). Constantine the Great declared the Sun his Comrade on empire-wide coinages and devoted himself to the cult until he adopted Christianity in its stead.

Though Roman religion never produced a comprehensive code of conduct, its early rituals of house and farm engendered a feeling of duty and unity. Its idea of reciprocal understanding between man and god not only imparted the sense of security that Romans needed in order to achieve their successes but stimulated, by analogy, the concept of mutual obligations and binding agreements between one person and another. Except for rare aberrations, such as human sacrifice, Roman religion was unspoiled by orgiastic rites and savage practices. Moreover—unlike ancient philosophy—it was neither sectarian nor exclusive. It was a tolerant religion, and it would be difficult to think of any other whose adherents committed fewer crimes and atrocities in its name.

GODS AND GODDESSES

CHAPTER 3

AENEAS

Aeneas was the mythical hero of Troy and Rome, son of the goddess Aphrodite and Anchises. Aeneas was a member of the royal line at Troy and cousin of Hector. He played a prominent part in the war to defend his city against the Greeks, being second only to Hector in ability. Homer implies that Aeneas did not like his subordinate position, and from that suggestion arose a later tradition that Aeneas helped to betray Troy to the Greeks. The more common version, however, made Aeneas the leader of the Trojan survivors after Troy was taken by the Greeks. In any case, Aeneas survived the war, and his figure was thus available to compilers of Roman myth.

The association of Homeric heroes with Italy and Sicily goes back to the 8th century BCE, and the Greek colonies founded there in that and the next century frequently claimed descent from leaders in the Trojan War. Legend connected Aeneas, too, with certain places and families, especially in Latium. As Rome expanded over Italy and the Mediterranean, its patriotic writers began to construct a mythical tradition that would at once dignify their land with antiquity and satisfy a latent dislike of Greek cultural superiority. The fact that Aeneas, as a Trojan, represented an enemy of the Greeks and that tradition left him free after the war made him peculiarly fit

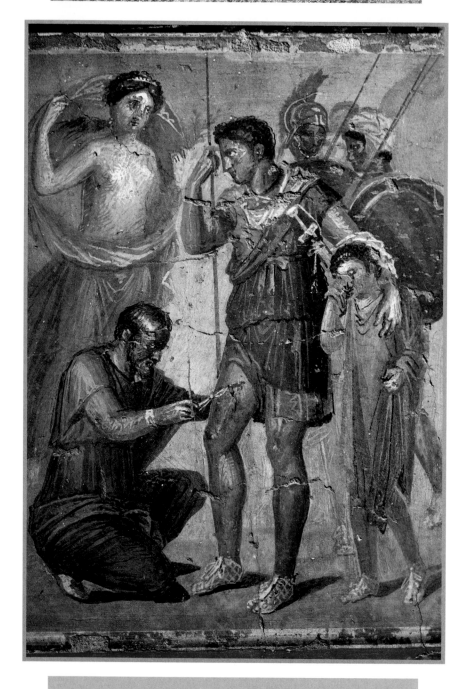

Fresco depicting wounded Aeneas. DEA/A. Dagli Orti/De Agostini/
Getty Images

for the part assigned him, i.e., the founding of Roman greatness.

It was Virgil who gave the various strands of legend related to Aeneas the form they have possessed ever since. The family of Julius Caesar, and consequently of Virgil's patron Augustus, claimed descent from Aeneas, whose son Ascanius was also called Iulus. Incorporating these different traditions, Virgil created his masterpiece, the *Aeneid*, the Latin epic poem whose hero symbolized not only the course and aim of Roman history but also the career and policy of Augustus himself. In the journeying of Aeneas from Troy westward to Sicily, Carthage, and finally to the mouth of the Tiber in Italy, Virgil portrayed the qualities of persistence, self-denial, and obedience to the gods that, to the poet, built Rome.

The *Aeneid* (written *c.* 29–19 BCE) tells in 12 books of the legendary foundation of Lavinium (parent town of Alba Longa and of Rome) by Aeneas after he left the burning ruins of Troy to found under supernatural guidance a new city with a glorious destiny in the West.

When Troy fell to the Greeks, Virgil recounts, Aeneas, who had fought bravely to the last, was commanded by Hector in a vision to flee and to found a great city overseas. Aeneas gathered his family and followers and took the household gods (small images) of Troy, but, in the confusion of leaving the burning city, his wife disappeared. Her ghost informed him that he was to go to a western land where the Tiber River flowed. He then embarked upon his long voyage, touching at Thrace, Crete, and Sicily and meeting with numerous adventures that culminated in shipwreck on the coast of Africa near Carthage. There he was received by Dido, the widowed queen, to whom he told his story. They fell in love, and he lingered there until he was sharply reminded by Mercury that

Rome was his goal. Guilty and wretched, he immediately abandoned Dido, who committed suicide, and Aeneas sailed on until he finally reached the mouth of the Tiber. There he was well received by Latinus, the king of the region, but other Italians, notably Latinus's wife and Turnus, leader of the Rutuli, resented the arrival of the Trojans and the projected marriage alliance between Aeneas and Lavinia, Latinus's daughter. War broke out, but the Trojans were successful and Turnus was killed. Aeneas then married Lavinia and founded Lavinium.

The death of Aeneas is described by Dionysius of Halicarnassus. After he had fallen in battle against the Rutuli, his body could not be found, and he was thereafter worshiped as a local god, Juppiter indiges, as Livy reports.

AESCULAPIUS

Aesculapius was the Greco-Roman god of medicine, son of Apollo (god of healing, truth, and prophecy) and the mortal princess Coronis. The centaur Chiron taught him the art of healing. At length Zeus (the king of the gods), afraid that Aesculapius might render all men immortal, slew him with a thunderbolt. Apollo slew the Cyclopes who had made the thunderbolt and was then forced by Zeus to serve Admetus.

Homer, in the *Iliad*, mentions him only as a skillful physician and the father of two Greek doctors at Troy, Machaon and Podalirius; in later times, however, he was honoured as a hero and eventually worshiped as a god. The cult began in Thessaly but spread to many parts of Greece. Because it was supposed that Aesculapius effected cures of the sick in dreams, the practice of sleeping in his temples in Epidaurus in South Greece became common. In 293 BCE his cult spread to Rome, where he was worshiped as Aesculapius.

Aesculapius was frequently represented standing, dressed in a long cloak, with bare breast; his usual attribute was a staff with a serpent coiled around it. This staff is the only true symbol of medicine. A similar but unrelated emblem, the caduceus, with its winged staff and intertwined serpents, is frequently used as a medical emblem but is without medical relevance since it represents the magic wand of Hermes, or Mercury, the messenger of the gods and the patron of trade.

APOLLO

Apollo was a deity of manifold function and meaning, after Zeus perhaps the most widely revered and influential of all the Greek gods. Though his original nature is obscure, from the time of Homer onward he was the god of divine distance, who sent or threatened from afar; the god who made men aware of their own guilt and purified them of it; who presided over religious law and the constitutions of cities; who communicated with mortals through prophets and oracles his knowledge of the future and the will of his father, Zeus. Even the gods feared him, and only his father and his mother, Leto, could easily endure his presence. Distance, death, terror, and awe were summed up in his symbolic bow; a gentler side of his nature, however, was shown in his other attribute, the lyre, which proclaimed the joy of communion with Olympus (the home of the gods) through music, poetry, and dance. In humbler circles he was also a god of crops and herds, primarily as a divine bulwark against wild animals and disease, as his epithet Alexikakos (Averter of Evil) indicates. His forename Phoebus means "bright" or "pure," and the view became current that he was connected with the sun. *See* Helios.

Among Apollo's other epithets was Nomios (Herdsman), and he is said to have served King Admetus of Pherae in the lowly capacities of groom and herdsman as penance for slaying Zeus's armourers, the Cyclopes. He was also called Lyceius, presumably because he protected the flocks from wolves (lykoi); because herdsmen and shepherds beguiled the hours

Fresco depicting Apollo with a lyre, as was appropriate to the god of music and poetry. Werner Forman/Universal Images Group/ Getty Images

with music, scholars have argued that this was Apollo's original role.

Though Apollo was the most Hellenic of all gods, he derived mostly from a type of god that originated in Anatolia and spread to Egypt by way of Syria and Palestine. Traditionally, Apollo and his twin, Artemis, were born on the isle of Delos. From there Apollo went to Pytho (Delphi), where he slew Python, the dragon that guarded the area. He established his oracle by taking on the guise of a dolphin, leaping aboard a Cretan ship, and forcing the crew to serve him. Thus Pytho was renamed Delphi after the dolphin (delphis), and the Cretan cult of Apollo Delphinius superseded that previously established there by Earth (Gaea). During the Archaic period (8th to 6th century BCE), the fame of the Delphic oracle spread as far as Lydia in Anatolia and achieved pan-Hellenic status. The god's medium was the Pythia, a local woman over 50 years old, who, under his inspiration, delivered oracles in the main temple of Apollo. The oracles were subsequently interpreted and versified by priests. Other oracles of Apollo existed on the Greek mainland, Delos, and in Anatolia, but none rivalled Delphi in importance.

Although Apollo had many love affairs, they were mostly unfortunate: Daphne, in her efforts to escape him, was changed into a laurel, his sacred shrub; Coronis (mother of Asclepius) was shot by Apollo's twin, Artemis, when Coronis proved unfaithful; and Cassandra (daughter of King Priam of Troy) rejected his advances and was punished by being made to utter true prophecies that no one believed.

In Italy Apollo was introduced at an early date and was primarily concerned, as in Greece, with healing and prophecy; he was highly revered by the emperor Augustus because the Battle of Actium (31 BCE) was fought near one of his temples. In art Apollo was represented as a beardless youth, either naked or robed, and often holding either a bow or a lyre.

ATLAS

Atlas was the son of the Titan Iapetus and the Oceanid Clymene (or Asia) and brother of Prometheus (creator of humankind). In Homer's *Odyssey*, Book I, Atlas seems to have been a marine creature who supported the pillars that held heaven and Earth apart. These were thought to rest in the sea immediately beyond the most western horizon, but later the name of Atlas was transferred to a range of mountains in northwestern Africa.

Fifth-century BCE *statue of Atlas from the Temple of the Olympian Zeus in Agrigento, Sicily.* DEA /G. Nimatallah/De Agostini/ Getty Images

Atlas was subsequently represented as the king of that district, turned into a rocky mountain by the hero Perseus, who, to punish Atlas for his inhospitality, showed him the Gorgon's head, the sight of which turned men to stone. According to Hesiod's *Theogony*, Atlas was one of the Titans who took part in their war against Zeus, for which as a punishment he was condemned to hold aloft the heavens. In many works of art he was represented as carrying the heavens (in Classical art from the 6th century BCE) or the celestial globe (in Hellenistic and Roman art).

AURORA

In Greco-Roman mythology, Aurora was the personification of the dawn. According to the Greek poet Hesiod's *Theogony*, she was the daughter of the Titan Hyperion and the Titaness Theia and sister of Helios, the sun god, and Selene, the moon goddess. By the Titan Astraeus she was the mother of the winds Zephyrus, Notus, and Boreas, and of Hesperus (the Evening Star) and the other stars; by Tithonus of Assyria she was the mother of Memnon, king of the Ethiopians, who was slain by Achilles at Troy. She bears in Homer's works the epithet Rosy-Fingered.

Eos was also represented as the lover of the hunter Orion and of the youthful hunter Cephalus, by whom she

VENERATION OF OBJECTS IN ROMAN RELIGION

Certain objects in Roman religion inspired a belief that they were in some way more than natural. This feeling was aroused, for example, by springs and woods, objects of gratitude in the torrid summer, or by stones that were often believed to be meteorites—i.e., had apparently reached Earth in an uncanny fashion. To these were added products of human action, such as burial places and boundary stones, and inexplicable things, such as Neolithic implements (probably the mysterious meteorites were often these) or bronze shields (artifacts that had strayed in from more advanced cultures).

was the mother of Phaethon (not the same as the son of Helios). Her most famous lover was the Trojan Tithonus, for whom she gained from Zeus the gift of immortality but forgot to ask for eternal youth. As a result, Tithonus grew ever older and weaker, but he could not die. In works of art Eos is represented as a young woman, usually winged, either walking fast with a youth in her arms or rising from the sea in a chariot drawn by winged horses; sometimes, as the goddess who dispenses the dews of the morning, she has a pitcher in each hand.

In Latin writings the name Aurora was used (e.g., by Virgil) for the east.

BACCHUS

In Roman literature Bacchus is often misunderstood, and he is simplistically portrayed as the jolly god who is invoked at drinking parties. In Greco-Roman religion, Bacchus, also known as Dionysus, was a nature god of fruitfulness and vegetation, especially known as a god of wine and ecstasy. The occurrence of his name on a Linear B tablet (13th century BCE) shows that he was already worshipped in the Mycenaean period, although it is not known where his cult originated. In all the legends of his cult, he is depicted as having foreign origins.

Dionysus was the son of Zeus and Semele, a daughter of Cadmus (king of Thebes). Out of jealousy, Hera, the wife of Zeus, persuaded the pregnant Semele to prove her lover's divinity by requesting that he appear in his real person. Zeus complied, but his power was too great for the mortal Semele, who was blasted with thunderbolts. However, Zeus saved his son by sewing him up in his thigh and keeping him there until he reached maturity, so he was twice born. Dionysus was then conveyed by the god Hermes to be brought up by the bacchantes (maenads, or thyiads) of Nysa, a purely imaginary spot.

As Dionysus apparently represented the sap, juice, or lifeblood element in nature, lavish festal orgia (rites) in his honour were widely instituted. These Dionysia (Bacchanalia) quickly won converts among women. Men, however, met them with hostility. In Thrace Dionysus was opposed by Lycurgus, who ended up blind and mad.

In Thebes Dionysus was opposed by Pentheus, his cousin, who was torn to pieces by the bacchantes when he attempted to spy on their activities. The Athenians were punished with impotence for dishonouring the god's cult. Their husbands' resistance notwithstanding, women took to the hills, wearing fawn skins and crowns of ivy and shouting the ritual cry, "Euoi!" Forming thyai (holy bands) and waving thyrsoi (singular: thyrsus; fennel wands bound with grapevine and tipped with ivy), they danced by torchlight to the rhythm of the aulos (double pipe) and thetympanon (handheld drum). While they were under the god's inspiration, the bacchantes were believed to possess occult powers and the ability to charm snakes and suckle animals, as well as preternatural strength that enabled them to tear living victims to pieces before indulging in a ritual feast (omophagia).

Marble sarcophagus depicting Bacchus and Ariadne, located in the Ny Carlsberg Glyptotek museum in Copenhagen, Denmark. Prisma/ Universal Images Group/Getty Images

The bacchantes hailed the god by his titles of Bromios ("Thunderer"), Taurokeros ("Bull-Horned"), or Tauroprosopos ("Bull-Faced"), in the belief that he incarnated the sacrificial beast.

In Orphic legend (i.e., based on the stories of Orpheus) Dionysus—under the name Zagreus—was the son of Zeus by his daughter Persephone. At the direction of Hera, the infant Zagreus/Dionysus was torn to pieces, cooked, and eaten by the evil Titans. But his heart was saved by Athena, and he (now Dionysus) was resurrected by Zeus through Semele. Zeus struck the Titans with lightning, and they were consumed by fire. From their ashes came the first men, who thus possessed both the evil nature of the Titans and the divine nature of the gods.

Dionysus had the power to inspire and to create ecstasy, and his cult had special importance for art and literature. Performances of tragedy and comedy in Athens were part of two festivals of Dionysus, the Lenaea and the Great (or City) Dionysia. He was also honoured in lyric poems called dithyrambs.

The followers of Dionysus included spirits of fertility, such as thesatyrs and sileni, and in his rituals the phallus was prominent. He often took on a bestial shape and was associated with various animals. His personal attributes were an ivy wreath, the thyrsus, and the kantharos, a large two-handled goblet. In early art he was represented as a bearded man, but later he was portrayed as youthful and effeminate. Bacchic revels were a favourite subject of vase painters.

BELLONA

Bellona was, in Roman religion, goddess of war, identified with the Greek Enyo. Sometimes known as the sister or wife of Mars, she has also been identified with his female cult partner Nerio. Her temple at Rome stood in the Campus Martius, outside the city's gates near the Circus Flaminius and the temple of Apollo. There the Senate met to discuss generals' claims to triumphs and to receive foreign ambassadors. In front of it was the columna bellica, where the ceremony of declaring war by the fetiales (a group of priestly officials) took place.

CERBERUS

Cerberus was the monstrous watchdog of the underworld. He was usually said to have three heads, though the poet Hesiod (flourished 7th century BCE) said he had 50. Heads of snakes grew from his back, and he had a serpent's tail. He devoured anyone who tried to escape the kingdom of Hades, the lord of the underworld, and he refused entrance to living humans, though the mythic hero Orpheus gained passage by charming him with music. One of the labours of the warrior Heracles was to bring Cerberus up to the land of the living; after succeeding, he returned the creature to Hades.

CERES

In Roman religion, Ceres was the goddess of the growth of food plants, worshiped either alone or in association with the earth goddess Tellus. At an early date her cult was overlaid by that of Demeter, who was widely worshiped in Sicily and Magna Graecia. On the advice of the Sibylline Books, a cult of Ceres, Liber, and Libera was introduced into Rome (according to tradition, in 496 BCE) to check a famine. The temple, built on the Aventine Hill in 493 BCE, became a centre of plebeian religious and political activities and also became known for the splendour of its works of art. Destroyed by fire in 31 BCE, it was restored by Augustus. The three chief festivals of Ceres's cult all followed Greek lines.

CLEMENTIA

Clementia, in Roman religion, was the personification of mercy and clemency. Her worship began with her deification as the celebrated virtue of Julius Caesar. The Senate in 44 BCE decreed a temple to Caesar and Clementia, in which the cult statue represented the two figures clasping hands. Tiberius was honoured with an altar to his clementia, and the clemency of Caligula received yearly sacrifices. On coins the goddess was usually depicted standing, with a patera (a dish used in sacrifices) in one hand and a sceptre in the other.

CONCORDIA

In Roman religion, Concordia was a goddess who was the personification of "concord," or "agreement," especially among members or classes of the Roman state. She had several temples at Rome; the oldest and most important one was located in the Forum at the end of the Via Sacra ("Sacred Way"). After 121 BCE, when the construction of the largest temple was ordered, the Senate frequently met at the temple in times of public uproar. The temple was restored under the emperor Augustus by his eventual successor, Tiberius, in 7 BCE. Tiberius placed many works of art there, and the temple became a kind of museum and tourist attraction during the Roman Empire. Concordia often appeared on coins as a matron holding a cornucopia in her left hand and either an olive branch or a patera (a dish used in sacrifices) in her right.

CUPID

Cupid was the ancient Roman god of love in all its varieties, the counterpart of the Greek god Eros and the equivalent of Amor in Latin poetry. According to myth, Cupid was the son of Mercury, the winged messenger of the gods, and Venus, the goddess of love. He often appeared as a winged infant carrying a bow and a quiver of arrows whose wounds inspired love or passion in his every victim. He was sometimes portrayed wearing

Fresco depicting Cupid hunting a hare, located in Pompeii, Italy. DEA/G. Dagli Orti/De Agostini/Getty Images

armour like that of Mars, the god of war, perhaps to suggest ironic parallels between warfare and romance or to symbolize the invincibility of love.

Although some literature portrayed Cupid as callous and careless, he was generally viewed as beneficent, on account of the happiness he imparted to couples both mortal and immortal. At the worst he was considered mischievous in his matchmaking, this mischief often directed by his mother, Venus. In one tale, her machinations backfired when she used Cupid in revenge on the mortal Psyche, only to have Cupid fall in love and succeed in making Psyche his immortal wife.

THE PURPOSE OF SACRIFICE AND MAGIC

In order to secure their food supply, physical protection, and growth in numbers, the early Romans believed that the gods had to be propitiated and made allies. Sacrifice was necessary. The product sacrificed would revitalize the divinity, which was seen as a power of action and therefore likely to run down unless so revitalized. By this nourishment he or it would become able and ready to fulfill requests. And so the sacrifice was accompanied by the phrase "macte esto!" ("be you increased!").

Prayer was a normal accompaniment of sacrifice, and as a conception of the divine powers gradually developed, it contained varying ingredients of flattery, cajolery, and attempted justification; but it also was compounded by magic—the attempt not to persuade nature, but to coerce it. Though the authorities (e.g., c. 451–450 BCE, Law of the Twelve Tables) sought to limit its noxious aspects, magic continued to abound throughout the ancient world. Even official rites remained full of its survivals, notably the annual festival of the Lupercalia and the ritual dances of the Salii in honour of Mars. Romans in historical times regarded magic as an oriental intrusion, but Italian tribes, such as the Marsi and Paeligni, were famous for such practices. Among them curses figured prominently, and curse inscriptions from c. 500 BCE onward have been found in large numbers. There were also numerous survivals of taboo, a negative branch of magic: people were admonished to have no dealings with strangers, corpses, newborn children, spots struck by lightning, etc., lest harm would befall them.

CYBELE

Cybele, also called Cybebe, or Agdistis, was an ancient Oriental and Greco-Roman deity, known by a variety of local names; the name Cybele or Cybebe predominates in Greek and Roman literature from about the 5th century BCE onward. Her full official Roman name was Mater Deum Magna Idaea (Great Idaean Mother of the Gods).

Legends agree in locating the rise of the worship of the Great Mother in the general area of Phrygia in Asia Minor (now in west-central Turkey), and during classical times her cult centre was at Pessinus, located on the slopes of Mount Dindymus, or Agdistis (hence her names Dindymene and Agdistis). The existence, however, of many similar non-Phrygian deities indicates that she was merely the Phrygian form of the nature deity of all Asia Minor. From Asia Minor her cult spread first to Greek territory. The Greeks always saw in the Great Mother a resemblance to their own goddess Rhea and finally identified the two completely.

During Hannibal's invasion of Italy in 204 BCE, the Romans followed a Sibylline prophecy that the enemy could be expelled and conquered if the "Idaean Mother" were brought to Rome, together with her sacred symbol, a small stone reputed to have fallen from the heavens. Her identification by the Romans with the goddesses Maia, Ops, Rhea, Tellus, and Ceres contributed to the establishment of her worship on a firm footing. By the end of the Roman Republic it had

Marble bust of Cybele, located in Italica, Spain. DEA/G. Nimatallah/
De Agostini/Getty Images

attained prominence, and under the empire it became one of the most important cults in the Roman world.

In all of her aspects, Roman, Greek, and Oriental, the Great Mother was characterized by essentially the same qualities. Most prominent among them was her universal motherhood. She was the great parent not only of gods but also of human beings and beasts. She was called the Mountain Mother, and special emphasis was placed on her maternity over wild nature; this was manifested by the orgiastic character of her worship. Her mythical attendants, the Corybantes, were wild, half-demonic beings. Her priests, the Galli, castrated themselves on entering her service. The self-mutilation was justified by the myth that her lover, the fertility god Attis, had emasculated himself under a pine tree, where he bled to death. At Cybele's annual festival (March 15–27), a pine tree was cut and brought to her shrine, where it was honoured as a god and adorned with violets considered to have sprung from the blood of Attis. On March 24, the "Day of Blood," her chief priest, the archigallus, drew blood from his arms and offered it to her to the music of cymbals, drums, and flutes, while the lower clergy whirled madly and slashed themselves to bespatter the altar and the sacred pine with their blood. On March 27 the silver statue of the goddess, with the sacred stone set in its head, was borne in procession and bathed in the Almo, a tributary of the Tiber River.

Cybele's ecstatic rites were at home and fully comprehensible in Asia, but they were too frenzied for Europeans farther west. Roman citizens were at first forbidden to take part in the ceremonies—a ban that was not removed until the time of the empire. Though her cult sometimes existed by itself, in its fully

developed state the worship of the Great Mother was accompanied by that of Attis.

The Great Mother was especially prominent in the art of the empire. She usually appears with mural crown and veil, seated on a throne or in a chariot, drawn by two lions. (In some accounts, the lions were originally Atalanta and Hippomenes.)

Mother goddess figures are found in almost every ancient religion, but these figures, who were usually only goddesses of fertility and reproduction in general, should not be confused with the Great Mother of the Gods, who was regarded as the giver of life to gods, human beings, and beasts alike.

DIANA

In Roman religion, Diana was the goddess of wild animals and the hunt, identified with the Greek goddess Artemis. Her name is akin to the Latin words *dium* ("sky") and *dius* ("daylight"). Like her Greek counterpart, she was also a goddess of domestic animals. As a fertility deity she was invoked by women to aid conception and delivery. Though perhaps originally an indigenous woodland goddess, Diana early became identified with Artemis. There was probably no original connection between Diana and the moon, but she later absorbed Artemis's identification with both Selene (Luna) and Hecate, a chthonic (infernal) deity; hence the characterization triformis sometimes used in Latin literature.

The most famous place of worship for the Italian goddess was the grove of Diana Nemorensis ("Diana of the Wood") on the shores of Lake Nemi at Aricia, near Rome. This was a shrine common to the cities of the Latin League. Associated with Diana at Aricia were Egeria, the spirit of a nearby stream who shared with Diana the guardianship of childbirth, and the hero Virbius (the Italian counterpart of Hippolytus), who was said to have been the first priest of Diana's cult at Aricia. A unique and peculiar custom dictated that this priest be a runaway slave and that he slay his predecessor in combat.

At Rome the most important temple of Diana was on the Aventine. This temple housed the foundation charter of the Latin League and was said to date back

Second-century CE *marble statue of Diana, located in Italica, Spain.*
DEA/G. Nimatallah/De Agostini/Getty Images

to King Servius Tullius (6th century BCE). In her cult there Diana was also considered the protector of the lower classes, especially slaves; the Ides (13th) of August, her festival at Rome and Aricia, was a holiday for slaves. Another important centre for the worship of Diana was at Ephesus, where the Temple of Artemis (or Diana) was one of the Seven Wonders of the World. In Roman art Diana usually appears as a huntress with bow and quiver, accompanied by a hound or deer.

DIS PATER

D is Pater (Latin: Rich Father), in Roman religion, was the god of the infernal regions, the equivalent of the Greek Hades, or Pluto (Rich One). Also known to the Romans as Orcus, he was believed to be the brother of Jupiter and was greatly feared. His wife, Proserpina (a Roman corruption of the Greek Persephone), was identified with vegetation, being regarded as a goddess of death during her annual sojourn in the underworld and of abundance during her term in the upper regions.

Statue of Dis Pater. Marka/SuperStock

DISCORDIA

Discordia, in Greco-Roman mythology, was the personification of strife. She was called the daughter of Nyx (Night) by Hesiod, but she was sister and companion of Ares (the Roman Mars) in Homer's version. Eris is best known for her part in starting the Trojan War. When she alone of the gods was not invited to the marriage of Peleus and Thetis, she threw among the guests a golden apple inscribed "For the most beautiful." Hera, Athena, and Aphrodite each claimed it, and Zeus assigned the decision to Paris, then a shepherd on Mount Ida. Paris awarded the apple to Aphrodite, who then helped him win Helen of Troy. In the war that resulted, Hera and Athena remained implacable enemies of Troy.

FAMA

Fama, in Greco-Roman mythology, was the personification of popular rumour. Pheme was more a poetic personification than a deified abstraction, although there was an altar in her honour at Athens. The Greek poet Hesiod portrayed her as an evildoer, easily stirred up but impossible to quell. The Athenian orator Aeschines distinguished Popular Rumour (Pheme) from Slander (Sykophantia) and Malice (Diabole). In Roman literature she was imaginatively conceived: Virgil described her (*Aeneid*, Book IV) as a swift, birdlike monster with as many eyes, lips, tongues, and ears as feathers, traveling on the ground but with her head in the clouds. According to Ovid in the *Metamorphoses*, she inhabited a reverberating mountaintop palace of brass.

FAUNA

In ancient Roman religion, Fauna was a goddess of the fertility of woodlands, fields, and flocks; she was the counterpart—variously considered the wife, sister, or daughter—of Faunus.

FAUNUS

Faunus was the ancient Italian rural deity whose attributes in Classical Roman times were identified with those of the Greek god Pan. Faunus was originally worshipped throughout the countryside as a bestower of fruitfulness on fields and flocks. He eventually became primarily a woodland deity, the sounds of the forest being regarded as his voice.

A grandson of Saturn, Faunus was typically represented as half man, half goat, in imitation of the Greek Satyr, in the company of similar creatures, known as fauns. Faunus was the father of Latinus, who

Relief depicting Pan playing his pipes with a dancing maenad, a female follower of Bacchus, to his left. Werner Forman/Universal Images Group/Getty Images

was king of the Latins when Aeneas arrived in Italy. According to Virgil's *Aeneid*, Faunus told Latinus to give his daughter, Lavinia, in marriage to a foreigner—i.e., Aeneas. Like Pan, Faunus was associated with merriment, and his twice-yearly festivals were marked by revelry and abandon. At the Lupercalia, a celebration of fertility held partly in his honour each February in Rome well into the Common Era, youths clothed as goats ran through the streets wielding strips of goatskin.

FELICITAS

Felicitas was the Roman goddess of good luck to whom a temple was first built in the mid-2nd century BCE. She became the special protector of successful commanders. Caesar planned to erect another temple to her, and it was built by the triumvir M. Aemilius Lepidus. The emperors made her prominent as symbolizing the blessings of the imperial regime.

FIDES

Roman goddess Fides was the deification of good faith and honesty. Many of the oldest Roman deities were embodiments of high ideals (e.g., Honos, Libertas); it was the function of Fides to oversee the moral integrity of the Romans. Closely associated with Jupiter, Fides was honoured with a temple built near his on the Capitoline Hill in 254 BCE. In symbolic recognition of the secret, inviolable trust between gods and mortals, attendants presented sacrificial offerings to her with covered hands.

In the later Roman period, she was called Fides Publica ("Public Faith") and was considered the guardian of treaties and other state documents, which were placed for safekeeping in her temple. There, too, the Senate often convened, signifying her importance to the state.

FLORA

In Roman religion, Flora wasa the goddess of the flowering of plants. Titus Tatius (according to tradition, the Sabine king who ruled with Romulus) is said to have introduced her cult to Rome; her temple stood near the Circus Maximus. Her festival, called the Floralia, was instituted in 238 BCE. A representation of Flora's head, distinguished only by a floral crown, appeared on coins of the republic. Her name survives in the botanical term for vegetation of a particular environment.

Myths about her are recorded in Ovid's *Fasti*, Book V. A nymph called Chloris was kissed by the West Wind, Zephyrus, and was turned into Flora. This story is the subject of Sandro Botticelli's *Primavera*. According to Ovid, Flora helped Juno—who was angry that Jupiter had produced Minerva from his own head—become pregnant with Mars by giving her a magic flower.

FORTUNA

Fortuna, in Roman religion, was the goddess of chance or lot who became identified with the Greek Tyche; the original Italian deity was probably regarded as the bearer of prosperity and increase. As such she resembles a fertility deity, hence her

Nilotic mosaic of the flooding of the Nile River in Egypt, from the Sanctuary of the Fortuna Primigenia, located in Rome, Italy. DEA/G. Dagli Orti/De Agostini/Getty Images

association with the bounty of the soil and the fruitfulness of women. Frequently she was an oracular goddess consulted in various ways regarding the future. Fortuna was worshiped extensively in Italy from the earliest times. At Praeneste her shrine was a well-known oracular seat, as was her shrine at Antium. Fortuna is often represented bearing a cornucopia as the giver of abundance and a rudder as controller of destinies, or standing on a ball to indicate the uncertainty of fortune.

THE FURIES

The Furies, in Greco-Roman mythology, were the goddesses of vengeance. They were probably personified curses, but possibly they were originally conceived of as ghosts of the murdered. According to the Greek poet Hesiod they were the daughters of Gaea (Earth) and sprang from the blood of her mutilated spouse Uranus; in the plays of Aeschylus they were the daughters of Nyx; in those of Sophocles, they were the daughters of Darkness and of Gaea. Euripides was the first to speak of them as three in number. Later writers named them Allecto ("Unceasing in Anger"), Tisiphone ("Avenger of Murder"), and Megaera ("Jealous"). They lived in the underworld and ascended to Earth to pursue the wicked. Being deities of the underworld, they were often identified with spirits of the fertility of the earth. Because the Greeks feared to utter the dreaded name Erinyes, the goddesses were often addressed by the euphemistic names Eumenides ("Kind Ones") or Semnai Theai ("Venerable Goddesses").

86 Oreste tourmenté par les furies

Illustration depicting Orestes pursued by the Furie. Leemage/Universal Images Group/Getty Images

SACRIFICE AND BURIAL RITES

The characteristic offering of the Romans was a sacrifice accompanied by a prayer or vow. (The Triumph, associated with Jupiter, was regarded as a thanksgiving in discharge of a vow.) Animal sacrifices were regarded as more effective than anything else, the pig being the commonest victim, with sheep and ox added on important occasions. Considered best of all were the basic elements of life: heart, liver, and kidneys. Human sacrifice, on the whole, was extraneous to Roman custom, though its practice among the Etruscans may have contributed to the institution of gladiatorial funeral games in both Etruria and Rome, and it was resorted to in major crises, notably during the Second Punic War (216 BCE). Earlier in the century, and perhaps once before, a member of the family of the Decii had given up his life by self-sacrifice (devotio) in a critical battle.

Although ancestors were meticulously revered, there was nothing resembling the comprehensive Etruscan attention to the dead. In spite of elaborate philosophizing by Cicero and Virgil about the possibility of some sort of survival of the soul (especially for the deserving), most Romans' ideas of the afterlife, unless they believed in the promises of the mystery religions, were vague. Such ideas often amounted to a cautious hope or fear that the spirit in some sense lived on, and this was sometimes combined with an anxiety that the ghosts of the dead, especially the young dead who bore the living a grudge, might return and cause harm. Graves and tombs were inviolable, protected by supernatural powers and by taboos. In the earliest days of Rome both cremation and inhumation were practiced simultaneously, but by the 2nd century BCE the former had prevailed. Some 300 years later, however, there was a massive reversion to inhumation, probably because of an inarticulate revival of the feeling that the future welfare of the soul depended on comfortable repose of the body—a feeling that, as sarcophagi show, was fully shared by the adherents of the mystery cults, though, on the rational level, it contradicted their assurance of an afterlife in some spiritual sphere. The designs on these tombs reflect the soul's survival as a personal entity that has won its right to paradise.

GALINTHIAS

G alinthias was a friend (or servant) of Alcmene, the mother of Zeus's son Heracles (Hercules). When Alcmene was in labour, Zeus's jealous wife, Hera, sent her daughter Eileithyia, the goddess of childbirth, to sit outside Alcmene's bedroom with her legs crossed and held together by both hands with intertwined fingers—thus by magic delaying the delivery in order to foil Zeus's plans for the boy. Alcmene's labour continued for days until Galinthias, in some accounts aided by the Furies, tricked Eileithyia by announcing the baby's birth. The goddess, startled, unclasped her hands and jumped to her feet, allowing Hercules to be born. As punishment for this act, Hera transformed Galinthias into a weasel. The goddess Hecate, however, took pity on her and made her an attendant, and Heracles later built her a temple.

The story of Galinthias is told by the 2nd-century BCE Greek poet Nicander—whose version was preserved in a prose summary by the 2nd-century CE mythographer Antoninus Liberalis—and by the 1st-century CE Roman poet Ovid in Book IX of *Metamorphoses*. A different version of Heracles's birth appears in the 2nd-century CE work of the Greek geographer and historian Pausanias; in this telling, it was Tiresias's daughter Historis who fooled Eileithyia.

HERCULES

Hercules was one of the most famous Greco-Roman legendary heroes. Traditionally, Heracles was the son of Zeus and Alcmene, granddaughter of Perseus. Zeus swore that the next son born of the Perseid house should become ruler of Greece, but by a trick of Zeus's jealous wife, Hera, another child, the sickly Eurystheus, was born first and became king; when Heracles grew up, he had to serve him and also suffer the vengeful persecution of Hera. His first exploit, in fact, was the strangling of two serpents that she had sent to kill him in his cradle.

Later, Heracles waged a victorious war against the kingdom of Orchomenus in Boeotia and married Megara, daughter of Creon, king of Thebes. But he killed her and their children in a fit of madness sent by Hera and, consequently, was obliged to become the servant of Eurystheus. It was Eurystheus who imposed upon Heracles the famous Labours, later arranged in a cycle of 12, usually as follows: (1) the slaying of the Nemean lion, whose skin he thereafter wore; (2) the slaying of the nine-headed Hydra of Lerna; (3) the capture of the elusive hind (or stag) of Arcadia; (4) the capture of the wild boar of Mt. Erymanthus; (5) the cleansing, in a single day, of the cattle stables of King Augeas of Elis; (6) the shooting of the monstrous man-eating birds of the Stymphalian marshes; (7) the capture of the mad bull that terrorized the island of Crete; (8) the capture of the man-eating mares of King Diomedes of the Bistones; (9) the taking of the girdle of Hippolyte, queen of the Amazons; (10) the seizing of the cattle of the three-bodied giant Geryon, who ruled the island Erytheia (meaning Red) in

Fourth-century BCE *carrara marble bust of Hercules, likely in combat with the Nemean lion.* Prisma/Universal Images Group/Getty Images

the far west; (11) the bringing back of the golden apples kept at the world's end by the Hesperides; and (12) the fetching up from the lower world of the triple-headed dog Cerberus, guardian of its gates.

Having completed the Labours, Heracles undertook further enterprises, including warlike campaigns. He also successfully fought the river god Achelous for the hand of Deianeira. As he was taking her home, the centaur Nessus tried to violate her, and Heracles shot him with one of his poisoned arrows. The centaur, dying, told Deianeira to preserve the blood from his wound, for if Heracles wore a garment rubbed with it he would love none but her forever. Several years later Heracles fell in love with Iole, daughter of Eurytus, king of Oechalia. Deianeira, realizing that Iole was a dangerous rival, sent Heracles a garment smeared with the blood of Nessus. The blood proved to be a powerful poison, and Heracles died. His body was placed on a pyre on Mt. Oeta (modern Greek Oiti), his mortal part was consumed, and his divine part ascended to heaven. There he was reconciled to Hera and married Hebe.

In art and literature Heracles was represented as an enormously strong man of moderate height; a huge eater and drinker, very amorous, generally kindly but with occasional outbursts of brutal rage. His characteristic weapon was the bow but frequently also the club.

In Italy he was worshipped as a god of merchants and traders, although others also prayed to him for his characteristic gifts of good luck or rescue from danger.

HESPERA

Hespera, in Greco-Roman mythology, the evening star; although initially considered to be the son of Eos (the Dawn) and the Titan Astraeus, he was later said to be the son or brother of Atlas. He was later identified with the morning star, Phosphorus, or Eosphorus (Latin: Lucifer), the bringer of light (later discovered by astronomers to be the planet Venus). Hespera is variously described by different authors as the father of the Hesperides (the guardians of the golden apples) or of their mother, Hesperis.

HONOS

Honos was the ancient Roman deified abstraction of honour, particularly as a military virtue. The earliest shrine of this deity in Rome was perhaps built not earlier than the 3rd century BCE and was located just outside the Colline Gate on the north side of the city. A double temple of Honos and Virtus stood outside the Capena Gate on the south side. Originally a temple to Honos alone, built by Quintus Fabius Maximus Verrucosus (later called Cunctator) in 234 BCE, it was expanded by Marcus Claudius Marcellus near the end of the 3rd century BCE and contained many works of art that had been taken from Syracuse when Marcellus captured that city (212). Another temple, built by Gaius Marius, was located on the Velia, near Marius's house on the Via Sacra ("Sacred Way").

THE HORAE

In Greco-Roman mythology, the Horae (singular: Hora) were any of the personifications of the seasons and goddesses of natural order; in the *Iliad* they were the custodians of the gates of Olympus. According to Hesiod, the Horae were the children of Zeus, the king of the gods, and Themis, a Titaness, and their names (Eunomia, Dike, Eirene— i.e., Good Order, Justice, Peace) indicate the extension of their functions from nature to the events of human life. At Athens they were apparently three in number: Thallo, Auxo, and Carpo, the goddesses of the flowers of spring and of the fruits of summer and autumn. Their yearly festival was the Horaea. In Homer's *Iliad* they are the gatekeepers of Olympus. In the *Homeric Hymn to Aphrodite* they greet Aphrodite at her birth and accompany her to Olympus. They appear first in art on the François Vase (*c.* 570 BCE), which shows them attending the wedding of Peleus and Thetis. In the Hellenistic and Roman periods the Horae became the four seasons, daughters of the sun god, Helios, and the moon goddess, Selene, each represented with the conventional attributes. Subsequently, when the day was divided into 12 equal parts, each of them took the name of Hora.

JANUS

In Roman religion, Janus was the animistic spirit of doorways (januae) and archways (jani). Janus and the nymph Camasene were the parents of Tiberinus, whose death in or by the Albula River caused it to be renamed Tiber.

The worship of Janus traditionally dated back to Romulus and a period even before the actual founding of the city of Rome. There were many jani (i.e., ceremonial gateways) in Rome; these were usually freestanding structures that were used for symbolically auspicious entrances or exits. Particular superstition was attached to the departure of a Roman army, for which there were lucky and unlucky ways to march through a janus. The most famous janus in Rome was the Janus Geminus, which was actually a shrine of Janus at the north side of the Forum. It was a simple rectangular bronze structure with double doors at each end. Traditionally, the doors of this shrine were left open in time of war and were kept closed when Rome was at peace. According to the Roman historian Livy, the gates were closed only twice in all the long period between Numa Pompilius (7th century BCE) and Augustus (1st century BCE).

Some scholars regard Janus as the god of all beginnings and believe that his association with doorways is derivative. He was invoked as the first of any gods in regular liturgies. The beginning of the day, month, and year, both calendrical and agricultural, were sacred to him. The month of January is named for him, and his

Etruscan bust of two-faced Janus, located in Montalto di Castro, Italy.
DEA/G. Nimatallah/De Agostini/Getty Images

festival took place on January 9, the Agonium. There were several important temples erected to Janus, and it is assumed that there was also an early cult on the Janiculum, which the ancients took to mean "the city of Janus."

Janus was represented by a double-faced head, and he was represented in art either with or without a beard. Occasionally he was depicted as four-faced—as the spirit of the four-way arch.

JUNO

Juno, in Roman religion, was the chief goddess and female counterpart of Jupiter, closely resembling the Greek Hera, with whom she was identified. With Jupiter and Minerva, she was a member of the Capitoline Triad of deities traditionally introduced by the Etruscan kings. Juno was connected with all aspects of the life of women, most particularly married life. Ovid (*Fasti*, Book V) relates that Juno was jealous of Jupiter for giving birth to Minerva from his own head. After Flora gave her an herb, Juno gave birth to Mars.

As Juno Lucina, goddess of childbirth, she had a temple on the Esquiline from the 4th century BCE. In her role as female comforter she assumed various descriptive names. Individualized, she became a female guardian angel; as every man had his genius, so every woman had her juno. Thus, she represented, in a sense, the female principle of life.

As her cult expanded she assumed wider functions and became, like Hera, the principal female divinity of the state. For example, as Sospita, portrayed as an armed deity, she was invoked all over Latium and particularly at Lanuvium, originally as a saviour of women but eventually as saviour of the state. As Juno Moneta ("the Warner"), she had a temple on the Arx (the northern summit of the Capitoline Hill) from 344 BCE; it later housed the Roman mint, and the words "mint" and "money" derive from the name. According to Plutarch, the cackling of her sacred geese saved the Arx from the Gauls in 390 BCE. Her significant festivals were the Matronalia on March 1 and the Nonae Caprotinae, which was celebrated under a wild fig tree in the Campus Martius on July 7. Juno is represented in various guises. Most frequently, however, she is portrayed as a standing matron of statuesque proportions and severe beauty, occasionally exhibiting military characteristics.

Second-century marble bust of Juno, located in the Ny Carlsberg Glyptotek museum in Copenhagen, Denmark. Prisma/Universal Images Group/Getty Images

JUPITER

Jupiter, also called Jove, was the chief ancient Roman and Italian god. Like Zeus, the Greek god with whom he is etymologically identical (root diu, "bright"), Jupiter was a sky god. One of his most ancient epithets is Lucetius ("Light-Bringer"); and later literature has preserved the same idea in such phrases as sub Iove, "under the open sky." As Jupiter Elicius he was propitiated with a peculiar ritual to send rain in time of drought; as Jupiter Fulgur he had an altar in the Campus Martius, and all places struck by lightning were made his property and were guarded from the profane by a circular wall.

Throughout Italy he was worshiped on the summits of hills; thus, on the Alban Hill south of Rome was an ancient seat of his worship as Jupiter Latiaris, which was the centre of the league of 30 Latin cities of which Rome was originally an ordinary member. At Rome itself on the Capitoline Hill was his oldest temple; here there was a tradition of his sacred tree, the oak, common to the worship both of Zeus and of Jupiter, and here, too, were kept the lapides silices, pebbles or flint stones, which were used in symbolic ceremonies by the fetiales, the Roman priests who officially declared war or made treaties on behalf of the Roman state.

Jupiter was not only the great protecting deity of the race but also one whose worship embodied a distinct moral conception. He is especially concerned with oaths, treaties, and leagues, and it was in the

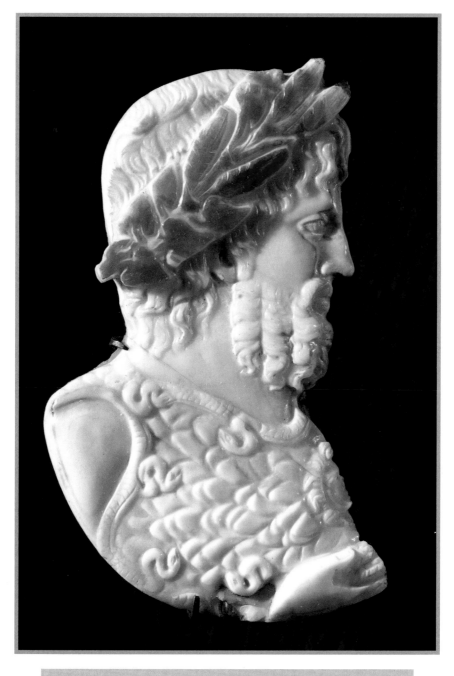

Sardonyx cameo, or carving, portraying head of Jupiter with a laurel and ivy crown. DEA/G. Dagli Orti/De Agostini/Getty Images

presence of his priest that the most ancient and sacred form of marriage (confarreatio) took place. The lesser deities Dius Fidius and Fides were, perhaps, originally identical and certainly were connected with him. This connection with the conscience, with the sense of obligation and right dealing, was never quite lost throughout Roman history. In Virgil's *Aeneid*, though Jupiter is in many ways as much Greek as Roman, he is still the great protecting deity who keeps the hero in the path of duty (pietas) toward gods, state, and family.

But this aspect of Jupiter gained a new force and meaning at the close of the early Roman monarchy with the building of the famous temple on the Capitol, of which the foundations are still to be seen. It was dedicated to Iuppiter Optimus Maximus (i.e., the best and greatest of all the Jupiters), and with him were associated Juno and Minerva, in a fashion that clearly indicates a Greco-Etruscan origin, since the combination of three deities in one temple was foreign to the ancient Roman religion, while it is found in both Greece and Etruria. The temple's dedication festival fell on September 13, on which day the consuls originally succeeded to office, accompanied by the Senate and other magistrates and priests. In fulfillment of a vow made by their predecessors, the consuls offered to Jupiter a white ox, his favourite sacrifice, and, after rendering thanks for the preservation of the state during the past year, they made the same vow as that by which their predecessors had been bound. Then followed the feast of Jupiter. In later times this day became the central point of the great Roman games. When a victorious army returned home the triumphal procession passed to this temple.

Throughout the Roman Republic this remained the central Roman cult; and, although Augustus's new foundations (Apollo Palatinus and Mars Ultor) were in some sense its rivals, that emperor was far too shrewd to attempt to oust Iuppiter Optimus Maximus from his paramount position; he became the protecting deity of the reigning emperor as representing the state, as he had been the protecting deity of the free republic. His worship spread over the whole empire.

JUVENTAS

In Homer the princess Juventas, daughter of Zeus and Hera, was a divine domestic, appearing most often as cupbearer to the gods. As the goddess of youth, she was generally worshiped along with her mother, of whom she may have been regarded as an emanation or specialized form. She was also associated with the hero-god Heracles, whose bride she became when he was received into heaven. Her major centres of worship were Phlious and Sicyon, where she was called Ganymeda and Dia.

LIBERTAS

Libertas, in Roman religion, was the female personification of liberty and personal freedom. Libertas was given a temple on the Aventine Hill about 238 BCE. (This is not the same as the temple of Jupiter Libertas restored by the emperorAugustus.) After the statesman and orator Cicero's exile (58 BCE), his political opponent the tribune Publius Clodius Pulcher built a small shrine to Libertas on the site of Cicero's house on the Palatine Hill; by consecrating the property to a goddess, Clodius was rendering it uninhabitable. When Cicero returned to Rome two years later, he argued before the Senate that the consecration was invalid. He eventually regained possession of the property and was permitted to dismantle the shrine. The Senate voted to build a temple to Libertas in honour of Julius Caesar in 46 BCE, but it was not built. A statue of Libertas was set up in the Forum. Libertas is usually portrayed as a matron with a laurel wreath or a pileus (a conical felt cap given to freed slaves, hence the symbol of liberty).

LIBITINA

Libitina, in Roman religion, was the goddess of funerals. At her sanctuary in a sacred grove (perhaps on the Esquiline Hill), a piece of money was deposited whenever a death occurred. There the undertakers (libitinarii) had their offices, and there all deaths were registered for statistical purposes. The word *Libitina* thus came to be used for the business of an undertaker, funeral requisites, and, by poets, for death itself.

Libitina was often mistakenly identified with Venus Lubentia (Lubentina), an Italian goddess of gardens. Libitina may have been originally an earth goddess connected with luxuriant nature and the enjoyments of life; because all such deities were connected with the underworld, she also became the goddess of death, that side of her character predominating in later conceptions.

LUCIFER

In classical mythology, Lucifer was the morning star (i.e., the planet Venus at dawn). Personified as a male figure bearing a torch, Lucifer had almost no legend, but in poetry he was often herald of the dawn. In Christian times Lucifer came to be regarded as the name of Satan before his fall. It was thus used by John Milton in *Paradise Lost*, and the idea underlies the proverbial phrase "as proud as Lucifer."

LUNA

In Greek and Roman religion, Luna was the personification of the moon as a goddess. She was worshipped at the new and full moons. According to Hesiod's *Theogony*, her parents were the Titans Hyperion and Theia; her brother was Helios, the sun god (sometimes called her father); her sister was Eos (Dawn). In the *Homeric Hymn to Selene*, she bears the beautiful Pandeic to Zeus, while Alcman says they are the parents of Herse, the dew. She is often linked with Endymion, whom she loved and whom Zeus cast into eternal sleep in a cave on Mount Latmus; there, Selene visited him and became the mother of 50 daughters. In another story she was loved by Pan. By the 5th century BCE Selene was sometimes identified with Artemis, or Phoebe, "the bright one." She was usually represented as a woman with the moon (often in crescent form) on her head and driving a two-horse chariot. As Luna, she had temples at Rome on the Aventine and Palatine hills.

MARS

The ancient Roman deity Mars was, in importance, second only to Jupiter. Little is known of his original character, and that character (chiefly from the cult at Rome) is variously interpreted. It is clear that by historical times he had developed into a god of war; in Roman literature he was protector of Rome, a nation proud in war.

Mars's festivals at Rome occurred in the spring and the fall—the beginning and the end of both the agricultural and the military seasons. The month of March, which was named after him, was especially filled with festivals wholly or partially in his honour; the members of the ancient priesthood of the Salii, who were particularly associated with Jupiter, Mars, and Quirinus, came out several times during the month to dance their ceremonial war dance in old-fashioned armour and chant a hymn to the gods. October was also an important month for Mars. At the festival of the October Horse on October 15, a two-horse chariot race was held in the Campus Martius, and on October 19 the Armilustrium marked the purification of the arms of war and their storage for the winter. The god was invoked in the ancient hymn of the Arval Brothers, whose religious duties had as their object to keep off enemies of all kinds from crops and herds.

Until the time of Augustus, Mars had only two temples at Rome: one was in the Campus Martius, the exercising ground of the army; the other was outside the Porta Capena. Within the city there was a

Fifth-century Etruscan statue representing a warrior believed to be Mars. DEA/M.Carrieri /De Agostini/Getty Images

sacrarium ("shrine," or "sanctuary") of Mars in the regia, originally the king's house, in which the sacred spears of Mars were kept; upon the outbreak of war the consul had to shake the spears saying, "Mars vigila" ("Mars, wake up!").

Under Augustus the worship of Mars at Rome gained a new impetus; not only was he traditional guardian of the military affairs of the Roman state but, as Mars Ultor ("Mars the Avenger"), he became the personal guardian of the emperor in his role as avenger of Caesar. His worship at times rivaled that of Capitoline Jupiter, and about 250 CE Mars became the most prominent of the di militares ("military gods") worshiped by the Roman legions. In literature and art he is hardly distinguished from the Greek Ares.

There are several Roman myths about Mars. In one, Hera bore him, without Zeus, at the touch of a magic herb given her by Flora. In another, he was the father of Romulus and Remus by Rhea Silvia, a Vestal Virgin. Ovid, in *Fasti*, tells of Mars's attempt to seduce Minerva. In the only purely Roman myth, he is tricked into marrying the aged Anna Perenna.

MATER MATUTA

Roman religion, Mater Matuta was the goddess of the ripening of grain (although the Latin poet Lucretius made her a goddess of dawn). Her worship in Italy was widespread and of ancient origin. Her temple at Rome, located in the Forum Boarium, was discovered under the Church of St. Omobono in 1937. The oldest sanctuary there was built in the 7th century BCE. A small temple, first built earlier in the 6th century, was rededicated about 530 BCE; this temple was associated with Servius Tullius. The Roman historian Livy, writing in the early 1st century CE, tells that following the capture of Veii in 396 BCE, Marcus Furius Camillus rebuilt the temple. Livy also reports that the temple was burned down in 213 and rebuilt the next year. The archaeological record tends to support the literary sources.

The festival of the Mater Matuta (the Matralia) was held on June 11 and was marked by several unusual customs—among them that only free women in their first marriage might take part and that their prayers were not for their own children but for those of their sisters. The goddess was later identified with the Greek Leucothea, who in turn was identified with Ino, protectress of mariners. Thus Mater Matuta obtained an association with the sea that did not originally belong to her.

MERCURY

I n Roman religion, Mercury was the god of merchandise and merchants, commonly identified with the Greek Hermes, fleet-footed messenger of the gods. His worship was introduced early, and his temple on the Aventine Hill in Rome was dedicated in 495 BCE. There he was associated with the goddess Maia, who became identified as his mother through her association with the Greek Maia, mother of Hermes. Both Mercury and Maia were honoured in a festival on May 15, the dedication day of Mercury's temple on the Aventine.

Mercury is sometimes represented as holding a purse, symbolic of his business functions. Usually, however, artists borrow the attributes of Hermes irrespective of their appropriateness and portray him wearing winged sandals or a winged cap and carrying a caduceus (staff).

Ring depicting Mercury with his staff and winged sandals, located in the Museum of Fine Arts in Budapest, Hungary. Prisma/Universal Images Group/Getty Images

MINERVA

Minerva, in Roman religion, was the goddess of handicrafts, the professions, the arts, and, later, war; she was commonly identified with the Greek Athena. Some scholars believe that her cult was that of Athena introduced at Rome from Etruria. This is reinforced by the fact that she was one of the Capitoline Triad, in

Sardonyx cameo of Minerva, located in the Bibliotheque Nationale de France in Paris. Universal Images Group/Getty Images

PARCAE

Parcae, in Greek and Roman mythology, was any of three goddesses who determined human destinies, and in particular the span of a person's life and his allotment of misery and suffering. Homer speaks of Fate (moira) in the singular as an impersonal power and sometimes makes its functions interchangeable with those of the Olympian gods. From the time of the poet Hesiod (8th century BCE) on, however, the Fates were personified as three very old women who spin the threads of human destiny. Their names were Clotho (Spinner), Lachesis (Allotter), and Atropos (Inflexible). Clotho spun the "thread" of human fate, Lachesis dispensed it, and Atropos cut the thread (thus determining the individual's moment of death). The Romans identified the Parcae, originally personifications of childbirth, with the three Greek Fates. The Roman goddesses were named Nona, Decuma, and Morta.

association with Jupiter and Juno. Her shrine on the Aventine in Rome was a meeting place for guilds of craftsmen, including at one time dramatic poets and actors.

Her worship as a goddess of war encroached upon that of Mars. The erection of a temple to her by Pompey out of the spoils of his Eastern conquests shows that by then she had been identified with the Greek Athena Nike, bestower of victory. Under the emperor Domitian, who claimed her special protection, the worship of Minerva attained its greatest vogue in Rome.

NEPTUNE

In Roman religion, Neptune was originally the god of fresh water; by 399 BCE he was identified with the Greek Poseidon and thus became a deity of the sea. His female counterpart, Salacia, was perhaps originally a goddess of leaping springwater, subsequently equated with the Greek Amphitrite.

Neptune's festival (Neptunalia) took place in the heat of the summer (July 23), when water was scarcest; thus, its purpose was probably the propitiation of the freshwater deity. Neptune had a temple in the Circus Flaminius at Rome; one of its features was a sculptured group of marine deities headed by Poseidon and Thetis. In art Neptune appears as the Greek Poseidon, whose attributes are the trident and the dolphin.

PAX

Pax, in Roman religion, was the personification of peace, probably recognized as a deity for the first time by the emperor Augustus, in whose reign much was made of the establishment of political calm. An altar of Pax Augusta (the Ara Pacis) was dedicated in 9 BCE and a great temple of Pax completed by the emperor Vespasian in 75 CE.

PIETAS

Pietas, in Roman religion, is the personification of a respectful and faithful attachment to gods, country, and relatives, especially parents. Pietas had a temple at Rome, dedicated in 181 BCE, and was often represented on coins as a female figure carrying a palm branch and a sceptre or as a matron casting incense upon an altar, sometimes accompanied by a stork, the symbol of filial piety.

THE ROLE OF PRIESTS IN ROMAN RELIGION

Precedence among Roman priests belonged to the *rex sacrorum* ("king of the sacred rites"), who, after the expulsion of the kings, took over the residue of their religious powers and duties that had not been assumed by the Republican officers of state. Nevertheless, the hold exercised by the rex sacrorum and his colleagues was weakened by the Law of the Twelve Tables (c. 451–450 BCE), which displayed the secular arm exercising some control over sacral law. As late as c. 275 BCE the religious calendar was still dated by the rex sacrorum but by this time he was already fading into the background.

Very early origins can also be attributed to some of the flamines, the priests of certain specific cults, and particularly to the three major flamines of Jupiter, Mars, and Quirinus. Jupiter's priest, the flamen dialis, was encompassed by an extraordinary series of taboos, some dating to the Bronze Age, which made it difficult to fill the office in historic times.

Except for the rex sacrorum and flamen dialis, whose duties were unusually professional and technical, almost all Roman priesthoods were held by men prominent in public life. The social distinction and political prestige carried by these part-time posts caused them to be keenly fought for.

There were four chief colleges, or boards, of priests: the pontifices, augures, quindecimviri sacris faciundis, and epulones. Originally three, and finally 16 in number, the pontifices (whose name may recall antique tasks and magic rites in connection with bridges) had assumed control of the religious system by the 3rd century BCE. The chief priest, the pontifex maximus (the head of the state clergy), was an elected official and not chosen from the existing pontifices. The augures, whose name may have been derived from the practice of magic in fertility rites and perhaps meant "increasers," had the task of discovering whether or not the gods approved of an action. This they performed mainly by interpreting divine signs in the movements of birds (auspicia). Such divination was elevated, perhaps under Etruscan influence, into an indispensable preliminary to state acts, though the responsibility for the decision rested not with the priests but with the presiding state officials, who were said to "possess the auspices." In private life, too, even as late as Cicero and Horace in the 1st century BCE, important courses of action were often preceded by consultation of the heavens. The Etruscan method of divining from the liver and entrails of animals (haruspicina) became popular in the Second Punic War, though its practitioners (who numbered 60 under the empire) never attained an official priesthood.

Of the other two major colleges, the *quindecimviri* ("Board of Fifteen," who earlier had been 10 in number) sacris faciundis looked after foreign rites, and the members of the other body, the epulones, supervised religious feasts. There were also fetiales, priestly officials who were concerned with various aspects of international relationships, such as treaties and declarations of war. Also six Vestal Virgins, chosen as young girls from the old patrician families, tended the shrine and fire of Vesta and lived in the House of Vestals nearby, amid a formidable array of prehistoric taboos.

PROSERPINA

Prosperina (Greek: Persephone) was the daughter of Zeus, the chief god, and Demeter, the goddess of agriculture; she was the wife of Hades, king of the underworld. In the *Homeric Hymn to Demeter*, the story is told of how Persephone was gathering flowers in the Vale of Nysa when she was seized by Hades and removed to the underworld. Upon learning of the abduction, her mother, Demeter, in her misery, became unconcerned with the harvest or the fruitfulness of Earth, so that widespread famine ensued. Zeus therefore intervened, commanding Hades to release Persephone to her mother. Because Persephone had eaten a single pomegranate seed in the underworld, she could not be completely freed but had to remain one-third of the year with Hades, spending the other two-thirds with her mother. The story that Persephone spent four months of each year in the underworld was no doubt meant to account for the barren appearance of Greek fields in full summer (after harvest), before their revival in the autumn rains, when they are plowed and sown.

Fresco depicting Persephone, located in Magdalensberg, Austria. DEA/E. Lessing/De Agostini/Getty Images

ROMULUS AND REMUS

Romulus and Remus were the legendary founders of Rome. Traditionally, they were the sons of Rhea Silvia, daughter of Numitor, king of Alba Longa.

Numitor had been deposed by his younger brother Amulius, who forced Rhea to become one of the Vestal Virgins (and thereby vow chastity) in order to prevent her from giving birth to potential claimants to the throne. Nevertheless, Rhea bore the twins Romulus and Remus, fathered by the war god Mars. Amulius ordered the infants drowned in the Tiber River, but the trough in which they were placed floated down the river and came to rest at the site of the future Rome, near the *Ficus ruminalis*, a sacred fig tree of historical times. There a she-wolf and a woodpecker—both sacred to Mars—suckled and fed them until they were found by the herdsman Faustulus.

Reared by Faustulus and his wife, Acca Larentia, the twins became leaders of a band of adventurous youths, eventually killing Amulius and restoring their grandfather to the throne. They subsequently founded a town on the site where they had been saved. When Romulus built a city wall, Remus jumped over it and was killed by his brother.

Romulus consolidated his power, and the city was named for him. He increased its population by offering asylum to fugitives and exiles. He invited the neighbouring Sabines to a festival and abducted their women. The women married their captors and intervened to prevent the Sabines from seizing the city. In accordance with a

Fresco depicting Romulus and Remus being abandoned on banks of the Tiber River. DEA/A. Dagli Orti/De Agostini/Getty Images

treaty drawn up between the two peoples, Romulus accepted the Sabine king Titus Tatius as his co-ruler. Titus Tatius's early death left Romulus sole king again, and after a long rule he mysteriously disappeared in a storm. Believing that he had been changed into a god, the Romans worshiped him as the deity Quirinus.

The legend of Romulus and Remus probably originated in the 4th century BCE and was set down in coherent form at the end of the 3rd century BCE. It contains a mixture of Greek and Roman elements. The Greeks customarily created mythical eponymous heroes to explain the origins of place-names. The story of the rape of the Sabine women was perhaps invented to explain the

custom of simulated capture in the Roman marriage ceremony. By including Mars in the legend, the Romans were
attempting to connect their origins with that important
deity. In the early 21st century archaeologists discovered
remains from the 8th century BCE of a cave, possible
boundary walls, and a palace that demonstrated parallels
between history and legend.

The famous bronze statue of a she-wolf now in the
Capitoline Museums in Rome is believed to date to the
early years of the Roman Republic (late 6th to early 5th
century BCE); the suckling twins were added in the 16th
century CE. Some scholars, however, have claimed that
the statue is from the medieval period.

RELIGIOUS ART

A vast gallery of architecture, sculpture, numismatics, painting, and
mosaics illustrates Roman religion and helps to fill the gaps left by
the fragmentary, though extensive, literary and epigraphic record.
Starting with primitive statuettes and terra-cotta temple decora-
tions, this array eventually included masterpieces such as the *Apollo
of Veii*. Other works of art, more than 400 years later, include paint-
ings illustrating Dionysiac mysteries at Boscoreale near Pompeii, and
the reliefs of Augustus's Ara Pacis at Rome; and with the Christian
emblems of Constantinian sarcophagi and coinage a thousand years
of ancient Roman religious art comes to an end.

SALUS

Salus, in Roman religion, was the goddess of safety and welfare, later identified with the Greek Hygieia. Her temple on the Quirinal at Rome, dedicated in 302 BCE, was the scene of an annual sacrifice on August 5.

The augurium salutis, not involving a personification and possibly antedating the deification of Salus, was an annual ascertainment of the acceptability to the gods of prayers for the public salus. Because it was required to be performed on a day of peace, the constant warfare of the late republic caused its interruption, but it was revived by the emperor Augustus. In the empire, the goddess appeared both as Salus Publica and Salus Augusti. She was regularly represented on coins as Hygieia, with patera and sacred snake, or at times with ears of grain, symbolic of prosperity.

SATURN

I n Roman religion, Saturn was the god of sowing or
seed. The Romans equated him with the Greek agricultural deity Cronus. The remains of Saturn's temple
at Rome, eight columns of the pronaos (porch), still
dominate the west end of the Forum at the foot of the
Clivus Capitolinus. The temple goes back to the earliest records of the republic (6th century BCE). It was
restored by Lucius Munatius Plancus in 42 BCE and,
after a fire, in the 4th century CE. It served as the trea-
sury (aerarium Saturni) of the Roman state. Saturn's
cult partner was the obscure goddess Lua, whose name
is connected with lues (plague, or destruction); but he
was also associated with Ops, another obscure goddess
(perhaps the goddess of abundance), the cult partner of
Consus, probably a god of grain storage.

In Roman myth Saturn was identified with the
Greek Cronus. Exiled from Olympus by Zeus, he ruled
Latium in a happy and innocent golden age, where he
taught his people agriculture and other peaceful arts.
In myth he was the father of Picus.

Saturn's great festival, the Saturnalia, became the
most popular of Roman festivals, and its influence is
still felt in the celebration of Christmas and the
Western world's New Year. The Saturnalia was originally celebrated on December 17, but it was later
extended to seven days. It was the merriest festival of
the year: all work and business were suspended; slaves
were given temporary freedom to say and to do what
they liked; certain moral restrictions were eased; and

First-century CE fresco depicting Saturn, located in Pompeii, Italy.
DEA/G. Nimatallah/De Agostini/Getty Images

presents were freely exchanged. The weekday Saturday (Latin: *Saturni dies*) was named for Saturn.

SILVANUS

In Roman religion, Silvanus was the god of the countryside, similar in character to Faunus, the god of animals, with whom he is often identified; he is usually depicted in the guise of a countryman. Initially the spirit of the unreclaimed woodland fringing the settlement, he had some of the menace of the unknown. As clearings pushed back the forest, he evolved into a god of woodland pastures, of boundaries, and of villas, parks, and gardens. He never enjoyed a state cult or temple, but the simple ritual of his private worship at a sacred grove or tree had a universal appeal. In Latin literature his character tended to merge with that of the Greek god Silenus, a minor woodland deity, or Pan, a god of forests, pastures, and shepherds, and to be assimilated into the Greco-Roman mythological tradition.

SOL

Sol, in Roman religion, was the name of two distinct sun gods at Rome. The original Sol, or Sol Indiges, had a shrine on the Quirinal, an annual sacrifice on August 9, and another shrine, together with Luna, the moon goddess, in the Circus Maximus. Although the cult appears to have been native, the Roman poets equated him with the Greek sun god Helios.

The worship of Sol assumed an entirely different character with the later importation of various sun cults from Syria. The Roman emperor Elagabalus (reigned 218–222 CE) built a temple to him as Sol Invictus on the Palatine and attempted to make his worship the principal religion at Rome. The emperor Aurelian (reigned 270–275) later reestablished the worship and erected a magnificent temple to Sol in the Campus Agrippae. The worship of Sol as special protector of the emperors and of the empire remained the chief imperial cult until it was replaced by Christianity.

SHRINES AND TEMPLES

The Roman calendar, as introduced or modified in the period of the Etruscan kings, contained 58 regular festivals. These included 45 Feriae Publicae, celebrated on the same fixed day every year, as well as the Ides of each month, which were sacred to Jupiter, and the Kalends of March, which belonged to Mars. Famous examples of Feriae Publicae were the Lupercalia (February 15) and Saturnalia (December 17, later extended). There were also the Feriae Conceptivae, the dates of which were fixed each year by the proper authority, and which included the Feriae Latinae ("Latin Festival") celebrated in the Alban Hills, usually at the end of April.

Templum is a term derived from Etruscan divination. First of all, it meant an area of the sky defined by the priest for his collection and interpretation of the omens. Later, by a projection of this area onto the earth, it came to signify a piece of ground set aside and consecrated to the gods. At first such areas did not contain sacred buildings, but there often were altars on such sites, and later shrines. In Rome, temples have been identified from *c.* 575 BCE onward, including not only the round shrine of Vesta but also a group in a sacred area (S. Omobono), close to the Tiber River beside the cattle market (Forum Boarium). The great Etruscan temples, made of wood with terra-cotta ornaments, were constructed later and culminated in the temple of the Capitoline Triad. Subsequently, more solid materials, such as tuff (tufa), travertine, marble, cement, and brick, gradually came into use. Temple archives, now vanished, play a large part in the historical tradition, and the anniversaries of the vows to build the temples and their dedication were scrupulously remembered and celebrated on numerous coins.

SORANUS

Soranus, in Roman religion, was the underworld deity worshiped on Mount Soracte in southern Etruria. As priests, the hirpi Sorani celebrated a rite in which they marched barefoot over burning coals. Soranus was identified with Dis Pater, the Roman god of the underworld, or with Apollo, a Greek god adopted by the Romans, and had a female partner, Feronia, a goddess of uncertain attributes.

TELLUS

Tellus, also called Terra Mater, was the ancient Roman earth goddess. Probably of great antiquity, she was concerned with the productivity of the earth and was later identified with the mother-goddess Cybele. Her temple on the Esquiline Hill dated from about 268 BCE. Though she had no special priest, she was honoured in the Fordicidia and Sementivae festivals, both of which centred on fertility and good crops.

ULYSSES

Ulysses, known in Greek religion as Odysseus, was a hero of Homer's epic poem the *Odyssey* and one of the most frequently portrayed figures in Western literature. According to Homer, Odysseus was king of Ithaca, son of Laertes and Anticleia (the daughter of Autolycus of Parnassus), and father, by his wife, Penelope, of Telemachus. (In later tradition, Odysseus was instead the son of Sisyphus and fathered sons by Circe, Calypso, and others.)

Homer portrayed Odysseus as a man of outstanding wisdom and shrewdness, eloquence, resourcefulness, courage, and endurance. In the *Iliad*, Odysseus appears as the man best suited to cope with crises in personal relations among the Greeks, and he plays a leading part in achieving the reconciliation between Agamemnon and Achilles. His bravery and skill in fighting are demonstrated repeatedly, and his wiliness is shown most notably in the night expedition he undertakes with Diomedes against the Trojans.

Odysseus's wanderings and the recovery of his house and kingdom are the central theme of the *Odyssey*, an epic in 24 books that also relates how he accomplished the capture of Troy by means of the wooden horse. Books VI–XIII describe his wanderings between Troy and Ithaca: he first comes to the land of the Lotus-Eaters and only with difficulty rescues some of his companions from their lotos-induced lethargy; he encounters and blinds Polyphemus the Cyclops, a son of Poseidon, escaping from his cave by clinging to the

belly of a ram; he loses 11 of his 12 ships to the canni-
balistic Laistrygones and reaches the island of the
enchantress Circe, where he has to rescue some of his
companions whom she had turned into swine. Next he
visits the Land of Departed Spirits, where he speaks to
the spirit of Agamemnon and learns from the Theban
seer Tiresias how he can expiate Poseidon's wrath. He
then encounters the Sirens, Scylla and Charybdis, and
the Cattle of the Sun, which his companions, despite
warnings, plunder for food. He alone survives the ensu-
ing storm and reaches the idyllic island of the nymph
Calypso.

Detail depicting Odysseus (Ulysses) being tempted by the Sirens.
Leemage/Universal Images Group/Getty Images

After almost nine years, Odysseus finally leaves Calypso and at last arrives in Ithaca, where his wife, Penelope, and son, Telemachus, have been struggling to maintain their authority during his prolonged absence. Recognized at first only by his faithful dog and a nurse, Odysseus proves his identity—with the aid of Athena— by accomplishing Penelope's test of stringing and shooting with his old bow. He then, with the help of Telemachus and two slaves, slays Penelope's suitors. Penelope still does not believe him and gives him one further test. But at last she knows it is he and accepts him as her long-lost husband and the king of Ithaca.

In the *Odyssey* Odysseus has many opportunities to display his talent for ruses and deceptions; but at the same time, his courage, loyalty, and magnanimity are constantly attested. Classical Greek writers presented him sometimes as an unscrupulous politician, sometimes as a wise and honourable statesman. Philosophers usually admired his intelligence and wisdom. Some Roman writers (including Virgil and Statius) tended to disparage him as the destroyer of Rome's mother city, Troy; others (such as Horace and Ovid) admired him. The early Christian writers praised him as an example of the wise pilgrim. Dramatists have explored his potentialities as a man of policies; and romanticists have seen him as a Byronic adventurer. In fact, each era has reinterpreted "the man of many turns" in its own way, without destroying the archetypal figure.

VENUS

The ancient Italian goddess Venus was associated with cultivated fields and gardens and later identified by the Romans with the Greek goddess of love, Aphrodite.

Venus had no worship in Rome in early times, as the scholar Marcus Terentius Varro (116–27 BCE) shows, attesting that he could find no mention of her name in old records. This is corroborated by the absence of any festival for her in the oldest Roman calendar and by her lack of a flamen (special priest). Her cult among the Latins, however, seems to be immemorial, for she had apparently at least two ancient temples, one at Lavinium, the other at Ardea, at which festivals of the Latin cities were held. Hence, it was no long step to bring her to Rome, apparently from Ardea itself. But how she came to be identified with so important a deity as Aphrodite remains a puzzle.

That Venus's identification with Aphrodite took place fairly early is certain. A contributory reason for it is perhaps the date (August 19) of the foundation of one of her Roman temples. August 19 is the Vinalia Rustica, a festival of Jupiter. Hence, he and Venus came to be associated, and this facilitated their equation, as father and daughter, with the Greek deities Zeus and Aphrodite. She was, therefore, also a daughter of Dione, was the wife of Vulcan, and was the mother of Cupid. In myth and legend she was famous for her romantic intrigues and affairs with both gods and

Bust of Aphrodite, located in the Ny Carlsberg Glyptotek museum in Copenhagen, Denmark. Prisma/Universal Images Group/Getty Images

mortals, and she became associated with many aspects, both positive and negative, of femininity. As Venus Verticordia, she was charged with the protection of chastity in women and girls. But the most important cause of the identification was the reception into Rome of the famous cult of Venus Erycina—i.e., of Aphrodite of Eryx (Erice) in Sicily—this cult itself resulting from the identification of an Oriental mother-goddess with the Greek deity. This reception took place during and shortly after the Second Punic War. A temple was dedicated to Venus Erycina on the Capitol in 215 BCE and a second outside the Colline gate in 181 BCE. The latter developed in a way reminiscent of the temple at Eryx with its harlots, becoming the place of worship of Roman courtesans, hence the title of *dies meretricum* ("prostitutes' day") attached to April 23, the day of its foundation.

The importance of the worship of Venus-Aphrodite was increased by the political ambitions of the gens Iulia, the clan of Julius Caesar and, by adoption, of Augustus. They claimed descent from Iulus, the son of Aeneas; Aeneas was the alleged founder of the temple of Eryx and, in some legends, of the city of Rome also. From the time of Homer onward, he was made the son of Aphrodite so that his descent gave the Iulii divine origin. Others than the Iulii sought to connect themselves with a deity grown so popular and important, notably Gnaeus Pompeius, the triumvir. He dedicated a temple to Venusas Victrix ("Bringer of Victory") in 55 BCE. Julius Caesar's own temple (46 BCE), however, was dedicated to Venus Genetrix, and as Genetrix ("Begetting Mother") she was best known until the death of Nero in 68 CE. Despite the extinction of the Julio-Claudian line, she remained popular, even with the emperors; Hadrian completed a temple of Venus at Rome in 135 CE.

As a native Italian deity, Venus had no myths of her own. She therefore took over those of Aphrodite and, through her, became identified with various foreign goddesses. The most noteworthy result of this development is perhaps the acquisition by the planet Venus of that name. The planet was at first the star of the Babylonian goddess Ishtar and thence of Aphrodite. Because of her association with love and with feminine beauty, the goddess Venushas been a favourite subject in art since ancient times; notable representations include the statue known as the *Venus de Milo* (c. 150 BCE) and Sandro Botticelli's painting *The Birth of Venus* (c. 1485).

VESPER

Vesper, in Greco-Roman mythology, was the evening star. Although initially considered to be the son of Eos (the Dawn) and the Titan Astraeus, he was later said to be the son or brother of Atlas. He was later identified with the morning star, Phosphorus, or Eosphorus (Latin: Lucifer), the bringer of light (later discovered by astronomers to be the planet Venus). Hesperus is variously described by different authors as the father of the Hesperides (the guardians of the golden apples) or of their mother, Hesperis.

VESTA

In Roman religion, Vesta was the goddess of the hearth, identified with the Greek Hestia. The lack of an easy source of fire in the early Roman community placed a special premium on the ever-burning hearth fire, both publicly and privately maintained; thus, from the earliest times Vesta was assured of a prominent place in both family and state worship. Her worship was observed in every household along with that of the Penates and the Lares, and her image was sometimes encountered in the household shrine.

The state worship of Vesta was much more elaborate. Her sanctuary was traditionally a circular building, in imitation of the early Italian round hut and symbolic of the public hearth. The Temple of Vesta in the Roman Forum was of great antiquity and underwent many restorations and rebuildings in both republican and imperial times. There burned the perpetual fire of the public hearth attended by the Vestal Virgins. This fire was officially extinguished and renewed annually on March 1 (originally the Roman new year), and its extinction at any other time, either accidentally or not, was regarded as a portent of disaster to Rome. The temple's innermost sanctuary was not open to the public; once a year, however, on the Vestalia (June 7–15), it was opened to matrons who visited it barefoot.

The days of the festival were unlucky. On the final day occurred the ceremonial sweeping out of the building, and the period of ill omen did not end until the sweepings were officially disposed of by placing them in a particular spot along the Clivus Capitolinus or by throwing them into the Tiber.

In addition to the shrine itself and between it and the Velia stood the magnificent Atrium Vestae. This name originally was given to the whole sacred area comprising the Temple of Vesta, a sacred grove, the Regia (headquarters of the pontifex maximus, or chief priest), and the House of the Vestals, but ordinarily it designated the home or palace of the Vestals.

Vesta is represented as a fully draped woman, sometimes accompanied by her favourite animal, an ass. As goddess of the hearth fire, Vesta was the patron deity of bakers, hence her connection with the ass, usually used for turning the millstone, and her association with Fornax, the spirit of the baker's oven. She is also found allied with the primitive fire deities Cacus and Caca.

VULCAN

Vulcan, in Roman religion, was the god of fire, particularly in its destructive aspects as volcanoes or conflagrations. Poetically, he is given all the attributes of the Greek Hephaestus. His worship was very ancient, and at Rome he had his own priest (flamen). His chief festival, the Volcanalia, was held on August 23 and was marked by a rite of unknown significance: the heads of Roman families threw small fish into the fire. Vulcan was invoked to avert fires, as his epithets Quietus and Mulciber (Fire Allayer) suggest. Because he was a deity of destructive fire, his temples were properly located outside the city. In Roman myth Vulcan was the father of Caeculus, founder of Praeneste (now Palestrina, Italy). His story is told by Servius, the 4th-century CE commentator on Virgil. Vulcan was also father of the monster Cacus, who was killed by Hercules for stealing his cattle, as Virgil relates in Book VIII of the *Aeneid*.

GLOSSARY

atomism A doctrine that the physical or physical and mental universe is composed of simple indivisible minute particles.

Capitoline Of or relating to the smallest of the seven hills of ancient Rome, the temple on it, or the gods worshipped there.

conciliate To gain (as goodwill) by pleasing acts.

coup d'état The violent overthrow or alteration of an existing government by a small group.

ecclesiastical Of or relating to a church especially as an established institution.

envisage To have a mental picture of especially in advance of realization.

etymology The history of a linguistic form (as a word) shown by tracing its development since its earliest recorded occurrence in the language where it is found.

extant Still existing, not destroyed or lost.

geocentric Having or relating to Earth as centre.

Hellenization The act of making Greek or Hellenistic in form or culture.

humanism A doctrine, attitude, or way of life centered on human interests or values.

imperative Not to be avoided or evaded.

Julian Relating to a calendar introduced in Rome in 46 BCE establishing the 12-month year of 365 days with each fourth year having 366 days and the months each having 31 or 30 days except for February, which has 28 or in leap years 29 days.

magnanimity A nobility of feeling and generosity of mind.

monastic Resembling (as in seclusion or ascetic simplicity) life in a monastery.

monotheism The doctrine or belief that there is but one God.

Neolithic Belonging to an earlier age and now outmoded.

numismatics The study or collection of coins, tokens, and paper money and sometimes related objects (as medals).

oracle A person (as a priestess of ancient Greece) through whom a deity is believed to speak.

pagan A follower of a polytheistic religion.

plebeian A member of the common people of ancient Rome.

pontificate The state, office, or term of office of a pontiff, or bishop.

propitiate To gain or regain the favor or goodwill of.

prosaic Everyday; ordinary.

pseudoscience A system of theories, assumptions, and methods erroneously regarded as scientific.

Sabine A member of an ancient people of the Apennines northeast of Latium.

sarcophagus A stone coffin.

triumvir One of a commission or ruling body of three.

FOR FURTHER READING

Apollodorus, and Robin Hard. *The Library of Greek Mythology*. Oxford, England: Oxford University Press, 2008.

Bryant, Megan E. *Oh My Gods!: A Look-it-up Guide to the Gods of Mythology*. New York, NY: Franklin Watts, 2010.

Bulfinch, Thomas. *Bulfinch's Greek and Roman Mythology: The Age of Fable*. Mineola, NY: Dover Publications, 2000.

Buxton, R. G. A. *The Complete World of Greek Mythology*. London, England: Thames & Hudson, 2004.

Campbell, Joseph. *The Hero with a Thousand Faces*. Novato, CA: New World Library, 2008.

Campbell, Joseph, Bill D. Moyers, and Betty S. Flowers. *The Power of Myth*. New York, NY: Anchor, 1991.

Cotterell, Arthur. *The Illustrated Guide to the Mythology of the World: Ancient Greek, Roman, Egyptian, Norse, Chinese, Indian and Japanese*. London, England: Lorenz, 2011.

Day, Malcolm. *100 Characters from Classical Mythology: Discover the Fascinating Stories of the Greek and Roman Deities*. Hauppauge, NY: Barron's, 2007.

Green, Roger Lancelyn, Alan Langford, and Rick Riordan. *Tales of the Greek Heroes*. London, England: Puffin, 2009.

Hamilton, Edith. *Mythology: Timeless Tales of Gods and Heroes.* New York, NY: Grand Central, 2011.

Harris, Stephen L., and Gloria Platzner. *Classical Mythology: Images and Insights.* New York, NY: McGraw-Hill, 2012.

Homer, Richmond Lattimore, and Richard P. Martin. *The Iliad of Homer.* Chicago: University of Chicago, 2011.

Homer, Robert Fagles, and Bernard Knox. *The Odyssey.* New York, NY: Viking, 1996.

Leeming, David Adams. *The Oxford Companion to World Mythology.* Oxford, England: Oxford University Press, 2005.

Lenardon, Robert J., and Michael Sham. *Classical Mythology.* New York, NY: Oxford University Press, 2011.

Matyszak, Philip. *The Greek and Roman Myths: A Guide to the Classical Stories.* London, England: Thames & Hudson, 2010.

Nardo, Don. *Roman Mythology.* New York, NY: Lucent, 2012.

Thury, Eva M., and Margaret Klopfle Devinney. *Introduction to Mythology: Contemporary Approaches to Classical and World Myths.* Oxford, England: Oxford University Press, 2013.

INDEX